ADVANCE PRAISE

"The line between artist and art is ethereal. You are a team of exceptionally skilled artists, but your superpower is the way you open your process to allow others in. You invited us to contribute as you created. Like a troop of improvisational art school MBAs, you fed off of suggestions while guiding the efforts. You also made it so much more fun than it had any right to be."

—DAVID SIMON, SVP MARKETING, LUMINATE

"Focus Lab told us we would go on a journey together. It was the most delightful, creative and collaborative team I could have wished for. Thanks to your entire team for the incredible work!"

—SYDNEY SLOAN, CMO, SALESLOFT

"Establishing a brand that is equal parts human and enterprise-class in a saturated industry is no simple feat. We knew that going into this project. But Focus Lab put forth a team and process that immediately laid our anxieties to rest. Their capacity to translate the complexities of our mission, identity, and value prop into a beautiful, clean, and meaningful identity was simply outstanding. I could not be happier with the result."

—KENT SIRI, VP OF MARKETING, REIFY HEALTH

"You've totally spoiled us in terms of working with any other 'branding partner.' Why can't every team be like yours? Focus Lab has been such a valuable partner in this rebranding project. From the early days, they challenged us to look at our company differently, and they worked to truly understand our business despite the technical complexity. Other marketing firms I've worked with in the past either gloss over this or deliver immature content that requires a ton of rework. Not Focus Lab."

—MARIANNA NOLL, VP OF MARKETING, KION

"I've gotten thirty to fifty personal emails from people saying how impactful the new brand is and how awesome it is that we had the guts to rebrand."

—HUMBERTO AYRES PEREIRA, FOUNDER AND CEO, ROWS

"Focus Lab believes that a brand is not just built around the machinations of business but the heart and soul of the people that make up the business. It's not just what you are but why you are. Working with Focus Lab is like seeing a really good therapist. You talk it out. There are no 'yes people.' You are challenged, encouraged, inspired, and if you work the process, you'll come out on the other side not just with a better brand but a better company."

—TODD CALVERT, BRAND DIRECTOR, ZELLO

"Your process helped force us to resolve positioning hurdles a step at a time."

—BILL MOORE, CEO, ZELLO

"We knew from the beginning this wasn't going to be a simple ask, but you've somehow managed to capture the essence of this complex and evolving company."

—BRAD STELL, HEAD OF DESIGN, ASAPP

"Partnering with Focus Lab and investing in our brand so early in our journey has been one of the best decisions we've made. I can't tell you how frequently it comes up from recruiting prospects, sales calls, to applicants for open positions. We stand out."

—SKYLAR ANDERSON, VP OF DESIGN, APTIBLE

"The successful teamwork here was pretty near and dear to my heart. Today, we're smugly looking down the barrel of a damn successful rebrand. We started off on the right foot and never took that foot off the gas pedal."

—CRAIG CLARK, CMO, GALVANIZE

"I had very high expectations going into the project—needless to say, these were met and then some. Focus Lab engaged our whole team in the brand and messaging process, got to grips with our business quickly, and delivered a brand we're really proud of."

—TOM HACQUOIL, CO-FOUNDER AND CEO, PINPOINT

"More than all the actual work that was done, the process of collaborating with the experts at Focus Lab is what I valued the most."

—CHARLEY TODD, BOARD MEMBER, TED TODD INSURANCE

"Working with Bill and the fine, friendly folks at Focus Lab was a true highlight in our rebranding journey. Breaking news to no one: developing a whole new brand for your company is an emotional process! It requires an expert, steady hand. We hired Focus Lab because we could see they had a real passion for the art of branding and an attention to detail in their onboarding that we knew would carry over to our actual project. We weren't disappointed. The process was as frictionless as possible, and their team was always friendly, responsive, and engaged. It was a wonderful experience, and the quality of the work speaks for itself."

—MATT POWELL, CEO, BITWISE

"What I've found over the years in brand transformation work is that branding is as much about internal transformation as it is external. While the Focus Lab team excels creatively, the real magic comes through in the partnership and process of working through the challenging discussions and continuous iterations that it takes to get to the best outcome. They bring a level of collaboration and agility that, when combined with their creative talent, makes brand transformation a rewarding and engaging experience for everyone involved."

—SERGIO CLAUDIO, VP OF BRAND EXPERIENCE, ZUORA

"It was our great pleasure at Tighten to work with the fine folks at Focus Lab. It was truly a next-level experience. In addition to helping us breathe new life into our brand, the team put on a master class in client service. Being on the other side of the counter, so to speak, gave us a crucial new perspective on the client/agency relationship that is already informing our day-to-day work."

—DAN SHEETZ, CO-FOUNDER AND CEO, TIGHTEN

"Bill and the team at Focus Lab are second to none. The outcome for Tango was great (and that's important), but the journey and process to get there was galvanizing. We took on a rebrand at an earlier stage than most, and I'm glad we did. We now have the brand foundation to scale our product, customers, and team."

—KEN BABCOCK, CO-FOUNDER AND CEO, TANGO

"I worked with Bill on a brand redesign, and he not only exceeded my expectations, but I also became a raving fan! Every interaction with Bill and his team has been world-class. The level of detail and research that goes into each step of the process truly sets them apart."

—CHARLES E. (CHARLIE) GAUDET II, CEO, PREDICTABLE PROFITS

"MyWallSt partnered with Bill and the Focus Lab team for our recent rebrand. From the outset, it was obvious that the Focus Lab team was full of expertise, experience, and energy. They ran the whole process like clockwork, and we were delighted with the creativity and final designs. On a personal level, Bill is brilliant to work with and extremely pleasant and engaging."

—JOHN TYRRELL, CEO AND CO-FOUNDER, MYWALLST

"We took a long time to settle on a firm to handle an extensive rebrand. Bill and the team at Focus Lab stood head and shoulders above every other company we met with. Their process and deliverables far surpassed our expectations...leading us to a place we couldn't have even envisioned. I would pick them again for any job that overlaps branding, marketing, voice, UI/UX, etc."

—MIKE MASSEY, FOUNDER AND CEO, LOCALLY

"Where do I even begin? The Focus Lab brand support team was the linchpin to our rebrand rollout success. It took zero time for both the copywriter and designer to onboard and produce stunning solutions to wildly complicated concepts and requests. Besides the concrete and incredible work they produced, they radiated positivity. They met every challenge and concern with professionalism and optimism. I wish I could hire Focus Lab for everything related to marketing and brand. I was genuinely sad when I said goodbye to Stephanie and the Focus Lab team."

—ELIZABETH HAGUE, SENIOR DIRECTOR OF
BRAND AND CONTENT MARKETING, VERY

"The best experience with an agency I've ever had."

—ASTRID HATHAWAY, DIRECTOR OF MARKETING, BITOVI

"Bill and the Focus Lab team have the amazing ability to translate complex ideas into simple solutions that work across multiple mediums. I'm constantly blown away by the work Bill and the team produce. It has been an absolute pleasure working with them—we're already onto our next project together!"

—SCOTT BURGESS, CEO, CONTINU

"Simply put, Bill is a ROCKSTAR! Between JibJab and StoryBots, I have had the pleasure of working with Bill and the Focus Lab team on three epic projects. They knocked it out of the park on each one. I will admit that I am a complete snob when it comes to good design, and that's EXACTLY why I call Bill whenever we have an important job. In addition to their exquisite taste, they are also straight-up pros. The team is friendly and easy to work with, all of our projects were excellently managed, and they hit every goal we laid out. I honestly can't say enough good things about Bill, and I couldn't imagine working with anyone else!"

—EVAN SPIRIDELLIS, CO-FOUNDER, STORYBOTS, INC.

CONQUER YOUR REBRAND

AN INSIDER'S GUIDE TO SUCCESS

CONQUER YOUR REBRAND

Build a B2B brand that customers love and competitors envy.

BILL KENNEY

LIONCREST
PUBLISHING

CONQUER YOUR REBRAND

Build a B2B Brand That Customers Love and Competitors Envy

FIRST EDITION

ISBN   978-1-5445-3899-0 *Hardcover*
       978-1-5445-3898-3 *Paperback*
       978-1-5445-3897-6 *Ebook*
       978-1-5445-3900-3 *Audiobook*

A rising tide raises all ships. I dedicate this book to everyone in the brand industry, and to you, the reader, so that it may support you and your business in your rebrand journey.

CONTENTS

FOREWORD

BOB MOORE, CEO, CROSSBEAM

When a company grows, everything breaks. Over and over again. Communication, management, recruiting, compensation...you wind up perpetually revisiting each of them as you navigate each stage of growth and turn of the market. But what about your company's identity? If it lacks a strong foundation, it can break too—and the ripple effects can be far more dire.

Did a broken identity lead you to this book? Are you the one person who knows that your company's identity no longer works? No matter what brought you here, keep reading. The future of your business might just depend on it.

SPOILER ALERT: BRAND MATTERS

A lot of founders and investors talk about a company's "DNA" when speaking about its inherent strengths and weaknesses. In my early days as a founder, I thought the whole "company

DNA" thing was a fatalistic metaphor. Human DNA doesn't mutate over time, so how could a company do anything to improve theirs? I would eventually learn firsthand a company can evolve its DNA, but the longer you wait, the harder it gets—and the higher the stakes. My relationship with the visual identity of my companies has taught me this lesson more than anything else.

In my first company, RJMetrics, frugality was baked into our founding DNA. We were bootstrapped and proud, and ascribed a lot of glory to this mentality. My founding partner, Jake Stein, and I would argue over how many paperclips to buy, for instance, or whether or not to provide coffee at the office. Nothing was too small to squabble over.

We didn't start RJMetrics with the idea of selling groundbreaking software to large global companies. We wanted to find the best way to use our skills to create something the world needed. We pressed on with our lean mindset, happily measuring, identifying, iterating, and repeating.

Then something happened. Five years into existence, on the heels of a big VC investment, we were no longer incentivized to be frugal. Growth became our guiding trait. Our tech was pushing forward in big ways and getting a lot of attention. Funny enough, investors didn't care about our lean mentality. They wanted to know if we could grow faster.

We had to figure out what it meant to adopt a growth mindset that could make us a venture-scale company. Around this time, we realized we had skipped perhaps the most important part of a company's creation: defining who we really were. We had no identity, and therefore no brand. Without one, we had no value system or throughlines that would have allowed us to invoke a change in how we ran without losing the spirit of why we were here.

Dealing with these missing pieces created a herky-jerky, two steps forward and three steps back experience. As we grew, it became more difficult to iterate on a brand that wasn't really there. After all, our team was mostly made up of stubborn engineers. The idea of sitting in a room whiteboarding about our "brand identity" felt like, at best, a huge waste of time. Boy, were we wrong.

TRYING TO FIX A BUSTED FOUNDATION

At the early stages of any company, you either make foundational investments in brand, or you don't. By the time RJMetrics grew to a hundred employees, we'd hit an inflection point. There were more people than I could possibly know or influence on a personal level. Meanwhile, new stressors revealed more and more cracks in our identity system. We overlooked everything related to values, mission, storytelling, visuals, you name it, and had no idea how to share what little we had in meaningful, inspiring ways.

To make up for it, my co-founder and I used ourselves like mascots, beating various drums in hopes that others would figure us out. (We were the "R" and the "J," after all.) This might work for bootstrapping a small business, but again, those days were over for us. The fact that we'd overlooked our brand identity was obvious. Weak points became fissures, and fissures became cracks. Our growth plateaued, and our value followed suit.

INVESTING IN BRAND EARLY

Dedicating time and resources to branding, especially early, can be a daunting proposition for anyone, but here's a pro tip: if you think you're going to get big (or if that's your ambition), then you have to think about brand identity early. Who are you? What is your value? What should your company look like? How do you make people feel? Do you know how to answer these questions and invoke them in your visual identity? The bad news for RJMetrics was that its founders, namely me, didn't appreciate this until it was very slow and expensive to fix.

Here's something else I discovered over time: We weren't really being lean by underinvesting in brand. We were being cheap, and it cost us in the long run. By the time we tried to solve for our weak brand, values system, and identity, we were already playing catch up, and we never truly caught up.

It's human nature to remember when you've been burned. As time goes by, you stay sensitive to repeating the same mistakes. The pain that my co-founder and I felt about RJMetrics is easy to access. We spent eight years building our company. When we sold, we were happy enough with the figure. Then, two years later, our top competitor sold for about a hundred times the amount we settled on. You read that right. We missed the billion-dollar version of our opportunity. When something like that happens, you don't ever stop wondering why.

We carried this scar tissue forward when we started our next company, Stitch Data. I would later bring the learnings with me to Crossbeam. In both instances, brand identity became table stakes on day zero. If we were going to build a product that people liked, and that would scale, we needed to launch with a long-lasting brand. With the help of Bill Kenney and his agency, Focus Lab, we got started early, and never looked back.

IT'S TIME TO CONQUER YOUR REBRAND

This work isn't easy, especially if you haven't gone through a legitimate brand or rebrand experience before. That's where *Conquer Your Rebrand* comes into play. This book peels back the covers on the entire process, then keeps going. It runs you through the highs and lows, gives you tactical insights and details, decodes insider language, and leaves you with actionable steps you can start using today.

One of the things I really enjoy about *Conquer Your Rebrand* is how Bill aligns the rebrand process with how Focus Lab works, without making you feel like you're in their sales funnel. It's more a case of Focus Lab standing in as an extended case study for how, when, what, and why.

Let me share this about my take on the branding process: I may no longer be a skeptic, but I still shudder a little at the soul-searching, "let's go have a vision quest" discovery phase. The thing is, it's critical to success, and this book does an excellent job showing how discovery and strategy continue to thread through the entire project.

As Bill points out, you need to be ready to go deep into who you are and what you're trying to accomplish. Knowing what drives and motivates your people and your business stirs the ground from where identity, brand, and every layer of narrative and visual language will eventually grow.

From early foundational inputs, to building vision and mood boards, to the final execution of story, logo, and more, *Conquer Your Rebrand* gets you ready for the step you're taking and the phases that follow.

Best of all, this book is a conversation. Bill and his agency are super easy to work with, and reading *Conquer Your Rebrand* is like having them across the table from you. They're masters at listening, then explaining what's what, why's why, and where the next step is. In that way, nearly every sentence in this book works like an answer to a brand-related question.

I'd like to wrap up by coming back to everyone's favorite acronym: ROI. Can you measure the ROI of doing brand right? I believe you can. Let me offer an example. When RJMetrics sold, our failure to invest in our long-term vision, or to build a public identity around it, contributed to us squandering the massive upside potential of our growing market, amazing people, good timing, and innovative product. With Stitch, where we invested in identity early, we set ourselves up to play big right away. With no incremental outside investment from venture firms, Stitch sold for $60 million cash two years after we launched. When you do the math on what we spent on brand, it wasn't a "a drop in the bucket," but a drop in the ocean.

Then there's Crossbeam. Four years in, we're backed by over $100 million of VC investment from firms I've admired forever. The work we put in early paints the picture, internally and externally, to inspire the confidence to bet big on our future. And it's working.

It doesn't matter what your position is right now—CMO,

founder, owner, or something else. If you believe in yourself, your people, and your company, and feel empowered enough to keep reading, then now is the time to push in the direction of building something big, and setting your company up to reach its true potential.

Let brand lead the way.

Robert J. Moore
CEO, Crossbeam

INTRODUCTION

The influence of branding is all around us, across all markets, businesses, and organizations. You interact with some level of branding every hour of every day. Sometimes you realize it, often you don't. That's a key feature and the superpower of branding.

Take a minute and think of some of the world's most influential organizations: Disney, Nike, Apple, Amazon, Coca-Cola, etc. They've understood this superpower for decades and are not shy about leveraging it. For winning organizations like these, the playbook always begins with the brand.

The value and impact of brand for B2C (business to consumer) businesses is clear, and has been for some time. But what is that impact for B2Bs (business to business)? Do the same rules apply? Are they completely different? Some people believe B2B brands should skew toward being pragmatic, serious, maybe even a little stodgy, while B2C brands get to have all the fun. They assume B2C is special and gets the freedom to do the "creative" stuff.

That thesis, however, is completely off course. Plenty of forward-thinking B2B companies agree. In the last decade, more and more B2B organizations have begun to focus on and invest in their brands. We see this investment and its resulting growth firsthand year over year in our work as a global B2B brand agency.

B2B organizations are becoming wise to the formula that B2C brands have capitalized on for years: When they lead with and execute consistently on brand, their momentum and opportunity for growth increase dramatically. Why is that? Before I answer, let me be clear—it takes more than just a brand to win. Still, great houses require strong foundations, and brand is that foundation, regardless of industry, customer segment, etc. That foundation serves as a powerful springboard.

B2B BRANDING MATTERS MORE THAN EVER

For nearly all organizations, and especially high-growth orgs, your most valuable intangible asset is your brand. I am referring to the things that are non-monetary, and non-physical—things you can't touch, yet still hold value. Tangible assets include things like the following:

- Your building
- Inventory
- Machinery
- Equipment
- Cash

On the other hand, intangible assets often include things like:

- Brand name
- Intellectual property
- Culture
- Processes
- Experience

While basic valuation is calculated by adding up all your tangible and monetary assets, the true total valuation of a company can't be fully understood without also considering the potential, and very real, value of your intangible assets.

The last decade has served as a pseudo turning point in the world of brand and branding. Industry-leading B2B companies have shifted their focus toward intangible assets, and are heavily investing in things like intellectual property, licensing, and brand. Why? Because they've come to understand that intangibles, specifically brand, are the glue that connects every piece of innovation capital.

> Innovation capital refers to explicit organisational knowledge residing in an organisation's intellectual property, business designs, business process techniques, patents, copyrights and trade secrets (among other factors) which enables organisations to build a competitive advantage either through economies of scale and scope or differentiation.[1]

This embrace of and investment in innovation capital increases the value of the tangible and intangible collectively beyond the sum of their parts. It turns out that organizations love a 1+1 =

---

1   HY Sonya Hsu and Peter P. Mykytyn Jr., "Intellectual Capital," *Encyclopedia of Knowledge Management*, IGI Global, September 2005, DOI:10.4018/978-1-59140-573-3.

3 scenario. Is Apple's most valuable asset the products it ships, or the ethos (brand) under which it builds them?

Considering your brand as an asset may be a new idea for you. However, if you take into account the impact that brand has on every touchpoint in your organization, both internal and external (customer loyalty, brand recognition and equity, internal culture and talent acquisition, etc.), it becomes clear how critical your brand is to your stickiness within your industry, your continued success, and, importantly, your valuation.

Research from McKinsey Global Institute shows a clear difference in outcomes between companies that invest in intangibles, such as branding, and companies that don't. Among tech, media, communication, and other innovation-driven sectors, the highest-growth companies invested 5.2 times more in intangible assets than their low-growth competitors.[2]

CHANGE IS HERE

If it's not crystal clear by now, your brand is a key ingredient in outperforming competitors in today's landscape. A new wave of business creation born from innovation is taking shape across the globe. B2B companies that get branding right have a unique chance to move to the front of an ever increasing line of business creation and competition. Those that get it wrong may wind up too far back to ever inch forward.

---

2   Eric Hazan et al., "Getting Tangible about Intangibles: The Future of
     Growth and Productivity?," McKinsey Global Institute, June 16, 2021, https://
     www.mckinsey.com/capabilities/growth-marketing-and-sales/our-insights/
     getting-tangible-about-intangibles-the-future-of-growth-and-productivity#/.

The days when companies could just throw new products or features at problems are long gone. Information is increasingly and easily accessible, and copycats are everywhere. Your competitors can replicate nearly every move you make—except for your brand.

Think of the brands you love and trust. Why do you trust them? Is it only their products and services? Or is it something else? Is their coffee (Starbucks) really that much better than the shop's down the street? Is their phone (Apple) truly superior to the competition's? Do you only use one rideshare app (Uber), even though the other promises the same results? Quite often, your choices come down to the fact that certain brands enhance everything around them: from creating a welcoming experience, to inspiring you to be braver, unique, world-changing, or better tomorrow than today. The point is this: brands and the behaviors around them are not rooted in reason but in emotion.

This is another area where many assume B2B is different from B2C—that emotion is not part of the equation. Surprisingly, in fact, the emotional connections in the B2B space may be even more important. One study by CEB Marketing, in partnership with Google and Motista, states that "B2B customers are significantly more emotionally connected to their vendors and service providers than consumers."[3] In other words, fortune favors the bold and the emotionally connected, regardless of customer base.

---

3   Sam Nathan and Karl Schmidt, "From Promotion to Emotion: Connecting B2B Customers to
     Brands," Think with Google, October 2013, https://www.thinkwithgoogle.com/consumer-insights/
     consumer-trends/promotion-emotion-b2b/.

In today's world, it should no longer feel impossible to imagine a B2B business taking on a big personality. Take Mailchimp for example. Intuit seems to agree: they acquired Mailchimp for $12 billion.[4] Mailchimp pulls no punches when it comes to their brand.

In my opinion, their brand's authenticity is infectious, and leaves zero confusion regarding who Mailchimp is, what they care about, and who they want to serve (not to mention that they don't need to wear a tie and use business jargon in order to impress their customer base). This is where self-awareness and courage come into play. With an inherently different *"feel,"* Mailchimp proudly stands as a refreshing juxtaposition to the old guard of B2B, and I'm confident part of that $12 billion paid by Intuit is for that *"feeling"* specifically.

Let's also consider the FutureBrand Index for a moment. This annual study looks at PwC's Global Top 100 Companies, orders them by market capitalization on perception strength, rather than financial strength, and interprets the rankings according to how brand resonant (future proof) these dominant companies are.

The 2021 index shocked a lot of people when it revealed B2B brands represented four of the top five brands for the year. The B2Bs? ASML Holdings, Prosus NV, Danaher Corp., and NextEra Energy.[5] Only Apple remained as the single consumer brand in the top five. This makes sense, since Apple is a master

---

4   Business Wire, "Intuit to Acquire Mailchimp," press release, September 13, 2021. https://www.businesswire.com/news/home/20210913005806/en/Intuit-to-Acquire-Mailchimp.

5   "The FutureBrand Index 2021 – The Top 100 Brands," FutureBrand, accessed March 15, 2023, https://www.futurebrand.com/futurebrand-index-2021/top-100.

at making a highly precise, tech-minded company feel like an approachable, trusted companion. And as the other four show, B2B can absolutely do the same. More importantly, your B2B company can do the same.

ACCEPTING UNCERTAINTY AND LETTING GO

Seeing data and facts is one thing. Actually building a B2B brand or engaging in an intensive rebrand is another. From our experience, one of the biggest obstacles that keeps B2B companies from building or redesigning their brand is uncertainty of the unknown, of change, and of being unable to see the opportunities at hand.

There is a ton riding on your brand. You're invested in your current brand, and you and your people are undoubtedly attached to it. A rebrand will cost you a fair amount of money. Plus there's all the assets to update, not to mention a nagging sense of uncertainty and a need for proof that what you're doing is going to work.

You're not wrong to think or feel this way, nor are you the first person to face this dilemma. But if you can see that the value you'll gain from a rebrand outweighs the risks of relinquishing your old brand; if you can remember that with every great return on investment there will always be an element of risk; if you can trust the data; and if you can see the opportunity standing in front of you, then *Conquer Your Rebrand* is the right book for this moment in your company's evolution.

This book draws the link between your company's brand, your position in the market, and what it takes to increase the value of your tangible and intangible assets, starting with a timely, strategic, and ultimately successful rebrand.

WHAT QUALIFIES ME TO WRITE THIS BOOK

Since 2009, when my business partners and I founded Focus Lab, our agency has been working to create the safe space and client-side confidence to turn complex brand challenges into quantifiable growth. To date, the numbers and results that we've helped influence speak for themselves:

- Eighteen unicorns: This is the number of our clients that have gone on to $1 billion valuations post-branding. Rebranding gave these companies the clarity of message and the consistency in application they needed to gain and maintain a distinct advantage in their space.
- More than five billion in capital: This is the total amount of capital our clients have raised following their brand work. The confidence gained when your brand now matches your company vision drastically increases the ability for others to believe in your vision with the same enthusiasm.
- Sixteen acquisitions, with more on the way: This is the number of clients who have been acquired following their rebrand. Organizations become much more attractive for M&A when it's clear that they have their act together, and your brand is the first place to begin establishing that credibility.

Our agency is humbled and proud of how many clients have risen to the point where they now lead and inspire their industries, unicorn or not. We want the same for your company. That's why, with the vast shared learnings of everyone who has passed through our doors, client-side and team members, I finally sat down to write this book to provide you with clarity, insight, and support across your rebrand journey.

A PLAYBOOK FOR YOUR REBRAND JOURNEY

Focus Lab exists to unlock the potential in the people around us. This book is another effort toward that mission. You wouldn't climb a mountain without a map, or without the help of an experienced guide. You shouldn't enter into a rebrand without the same type of support. I hope that's why *Conquer Your Rebrand* is in your hands.

My goal is to filter our decades-plus of B2B rebranding experiences through an authentic, no-strings-attached, insider lens resulting in clear action steps you can take as you set forth. This is a detailed, step-by-step playbook that by design spends only a short amount of time on why brand matters. It quickly shifts into providing you with value and pointing the way to navigating the rebrand process.

There are many books written on branding—more than twenty thousand, if Amazon's book search for "branding" is accurate. Very few of these books, if any, give you the insider look I'm about to share. I'm not here to convince you in a long-winded effort why you need to rebrand. Instead, I'm here because you very likely understand the importance of brand but want a clear picture of the whats and hows involved in a rebrand:

- What is brand in its full definition?
- What will your rebrand involve down to the smallest details?
- How will things play out week to week in the actual work?

- How will it feel, and how should it feel, when you're going through the rebrand experience?

As you progress from chapter to chapter, *Conquer Your Rebrand* will also serve as your guide to help you answer the ever-growing list of the questions you either have already or that arise along your journey. Some of those questions will include:

- How will I know if a rebrand is what I need?
- What should I consider when looking for an agency partner?
- How will I involve stakeholders in this journey?
- How do I know if I will lose/gain equity in a rebrand?
- How can I ensure I won't end up with a brand that I hate?
- How long will it take, and how much effort is needed on my side?
- Should I poll my customers on how they feel about the work?
- How can I make the biggest splash possible on rollout?
- And about a million other thoughts, fears, and curiosities.

My intention is to leverage the hundreds of unique projects, client personalities, team dynamics, and overall rebrand experiences into a single location to make your journey that much more effective. You'll capture a decade's worth of knowledge in a few weekends worth of reading.

NOW IS YOUR REBRAND MOMENT

Why are you reading this book? Why now? I suspect your organization has outgrown its current brand to the point where it no longer serves you. Your story is messy, or completely wrong. Maybe your brand never captured your mission. Maybe it was a placeholder but then never received proper attention. Maybe it speaks only to your customers but neglects your internal culture, which puts a damper on recruiting.

Your business is striving to reach new heights, but something is holding it back. Perhaps you've been relying on patchwork solutions (updating product features, putting more money into sales, etc.) without moving the needle. Has your vertical become oversaturated? Is your offering outdated? Questions keep coming, but where are the answers?

We believe the answer to what's holding you back isn't "out there" in the market. Instead, it's at the root of your business itself: your brand.

With hundreds of B2B rebranding efforts under our agency's belt, we still see a common trap: Companies place their "what" (product, marketing efforts, etc.) ahead of their "why" (brand). Author Simon Sinek, in his book *Start with Why*, makes a compelling case for how winning businesses are structured—a model he calls the "Golden Circle."

Sinek explains that any business that understands its "why" (authentic self and resulting story) is able to speak in a more connected way. This allows the business to reach its customer on a more emotional level. This is where leading businesses pull away from the competition, allowing their authenticity and relatability to rise to the top while shedding business jargon as the primary reflection of the business.

When a business chooses to start with features instead of purpose, it misses a critical step in the trust-building process wherein a customer builds a relationship first and makes a decision second. Making a simple shift (trust first, then choice) can create a big return.

You can't start with your "why" if you don't understand it first. That is the work of branding, and I'll share the steps involved in this process throughout the chapters that follow. Once you understand your "why," you can create a clear expression of it for your teams, and finally for customers. This idea forms the basis of one of our agency's mantras: Brand First. Brand Forever. It's a reminder that starting with your brand and clarifying your "why," are paramount for future success.

HOW THIS BOOK IS STRUCTURED

This book walks you through the rebrand journey in the following four-part cadence:

- **Part 1** (Chapters 1–3) focuses on the earliest aspects of the rebrand journey. It demystifies the nebulous word that is "brand" so we are all on equal footing before going further. You'll explore details that relate to knowing when it's time to rebrand, what a rebrand will (and will not) solve, and how to find and determine the right agency partner for your rebrand. Part 1 wraps with an extensive look at setting goals and expectations, right up through the onboarding process. By the time you finish reading Part 1, you'll have more confidence in your decision about whether to start a rebrand and a better understanding of how to get started.
- **Part 2** (Chapters 4–5) is a deep and critical dive into the pre-work that happens at the very start: building your team, meeting your agency's team, and kicking things off the right

way to ensure a successful process. Throughout Part 2, a number of foundational elements offer "how-to" logistical insights, and work toward creating a blueprint you can use to get off to a strong start.

- **Part 3** (Chapters 6–8) is where the rubber meets the road. This is what I consider to be the unique and most valuable aspect of this book. These chapters walk you through the actual project flow, including strategy, verbal identity, and visual identity. Part 3 draws from years of brand experience to provide insights into why certain things happen at different times, who's involved, and how each step leads toward the next.
- **Part 4** (Chapters 9–10) offers a safe landing out of the rebrand experience. These chapters cover the final steps involved in some of the critical details that you and your agency must dial in at the end, including exporting the right files, setting up and following through on your brand rollout plan, and getting the right post-project support to make sure nothing gets lost in the shuffle.

At the end of each of these four parts, you'll find an actionable list of takeaways that tie the previous chapters together and help you prepare for the stages that follow. The takeaways read like punch lists you can put to use right away as you prepare your team members and stakeholders for the work involved in your rebrand.

A DISCLAIMER ON TONE

In an effort to make this book as insightful as possible, I will lean into past experiences, some of which highlight the ways that clients occasionally stumble during a rebrand. If some sections feel like I'm telling you what to do, this tone comes from a place of support, not of judgment. My goal is to share common challenges, in order to help you avoid them during your own journey.

Also, you'll see references to "B2B" often. My agency is positioned in that market; it's the lens we look through, and the customers with whom we speak most often. Still, that does not limit the value of this book to the B2B space alone. At the end of the day, everything you read throughout *Conquer Your Rebrand* is fully applicable to any organization that's about to start the rebrand journey.

A NOTE ABOUT THE WORD "REBRAND"

Don't be thrown by the word "rebrand," especially if you haven't invested in brand before. This book will deliver the same value, regardless of whether you are branding a new company or rebranding an existing one. Most of our clients engage with our firm for a rebrand, and I'll use this lens to frame various points and perspectives. Still, my recommendations will hold true even if you are entering your first brand project.

A NOTE ABOUT YOU AND YOUR PROCESS

As much as I would love to assume that everyone reading this book will hang on and cherish every paragraph, sentence, and word, I know that's not reality. You will no doubt extract a personal level of value from the contents, as will every reader. Some readers will have had deep experiences in brand before, perhaps even having traversed multiple rebrands in the past. Other readers will be in the middle of a rebrand as we speak and looking for more immediate value by jumping to specific chapters. Some readers will have their own agencies and will be looking to borrow ideas. And naturally, some readers will have never conquered a single rebrand, and reading this book may feel like drinking from a firehose.

Wherever you are in your process, the good news is this: I've done my best to break points down into consumable portions. In the same way that our agency suggests not rushing a rebrand, I suggest not rushing this book. Whatever your situation may be, feel free to use this playbook as it suits you best. With that, let's begin the rebrand journey.

PART 1

CHAPTER 1

DEFINING BRAND

For this book to be as valuable as possible, I'd like to frame Chapter 1 as a moment and level-set what brand is and how our firm defines it. We have worked closely with hundreds of clients in varied markets since 2009. This has given us firsthand experience into the confusion and variations that occur when people try to define the meaning of brand. It's a notoriously difficult word to describe in a simple way that people can agree on. This isn't surprising considering how all-encompassing and intangible brand truly is. As I alluded to earlier, this is a feature of brand, not a bug.

As we dig in, I want to call on a mindset that Patagonia founder Yvon Chouinard discusses in his book, *Let My People Go Surfing: The Education of a Reluctant Businessman*. He reminds us that success in activities that require precision (archery, for instance), and the satisfaction you gain from monumental activities (climbing mountains) boil down to how much attention we give to the small steps along the way.

In other words, how we come out on the other side, and how we feel about it, depends on our attention to little moments that make up the big important one. Remember this as this book unfolds. Yes, a rebrand *is* a big project, but you don't have to take all of the steps or answer every question at once. If you diligently approach the work, and remember that each step is as important as the final outcome, you will reach the rebrand summit with a brand you are proud of.

GETTING CLEAR ON BRAND

What is brand? Is it your product? Your company mission? Is it your track record of success, or the paper used in your packaging? Is it the way you communicate or the core values of your organization? Is it the products you push out or the culture you celebrate within? Or is it what your customers say it is? The answer is yes—brand is all of the above and more. Your brand is the entire ecosystem around your company that leads to a feeling or perception in the eyes or hearts of your customers.

Consider Nike, a brand we all know. Regardless of how you feel about the company or their products, the Nike brand is a masterclass in execution. This fact has little to do with their logo and everything to do with their focus on all aspects of their brand. We can all identify the swoosh, which is the key purpose of Nike's famous mark. Beyond the swoosh, though, the Nike brand is rooted in the years of customers' experiences, product innovation, a bold voice, and alignment to human aspirations.

Nike's brand is also built on decades of powerful marketing, playing those same notes over and over again. These days, the Nike brand is also rooted and expressed in the social positions they take, like promoting inclusion and building communities. In the end, their brand continues to resonate because of their relentless consistency and an unwavering dedication to their mission: "To bring inspiration and innovation to every athlete* in the world."

Pay special attention to the asterisk in that statement. I didn't place it there—Nike did. They strengthened their position by adding extra emphasis on what it means to be an athlete within the Nike ecosystem, which reads as follows: "*If you have a body, you are an athlete."

That is branding, and a logo alone will never achieve that (nor is it supposed to). Still, a company's logo is often the first thing people think about when they think about brand, branding, or a rebrand. Our firm hears it time and time again: "Our company is changing, and we need a new logo." It's easy to understand why this line of thinking exists, particularly since so many companies place great emphasis on their logo. Unfortunately, this practice completely misses the larger and more valuable picture: on its own, your logo will never accurately express the true power of your company, regardless of how well it's designed. (I'll cover this in greater detail in Chapter 8.)

To change this perspective, I encourage people to think of brand the way you might consider an orchestra. It takes a full collection of instruments working in harmony to create a compelling sound. Similarly, your brand relies on multiple elements to add layer after layer of resonance, propelling your company's larger narrative in a way that connects with and inspires customers, followers, and fans. Interestingly, customers often cannot distinguish between the various moving parts, but they can easily identify how that brand makes them feel. Remember the definition of a brand is predicated on *feeling*. This makes the ROI of brand innately hard to measure. However, hard to measure doesn't mean that it isn't valuable. Customers *hear* the harmony and *feel* the feelings, even if subconsciously. That is the brand at work.

When a brand is collectively in tune, audiences recognize, relate to, and remember it. That recognition builds into understanding, alignment, and action. With this in mind, let's move to the next opportunity for clarity, and break down the difference between marketing and branding.

MARKETING AND BRANDING

Many people casually lump the terms "marketing" and "branding" together into a common definition, but they are not the same. Some go so far as to openly question things. "Isn't branding just a marketing exercise? Shouldn't the marketing budget determine how much we allocate to a rebrand?"

Branding and marketing share space and similarities, and both can struggle for relevance under the weight of amorphous definitions. In many cases, they complement each other so closely that one rarely exists without the other, but it is important to understand that they are different, and what that means for a branding effort.

The shortest answer is that branding is the necessary precursor to marketing. A brand is built on internal attributes that don't change, such as a company's values or vision. Branding is the construction of a company's brand. It is the proactive effort that a company takes to understand, distill, and crystallize its essence. The results of branding reflect who the company is, why it exists, what it aims to achieve, what it looks and sounds like, and much more.

Marketing is how a company leverages its brand, how it promotes its brand to the world and attempts to communicate to customers. It is directly influenced by the brand, in addition to other factors, and will change over time based on different conditions.

Here's one of my favorite concepts about the ways that marketing and brand overlap, and also how they differ. Brand is the pull, and marketing is the push. Brand is the offer; marketing is the promotion of that offer.

Without branding, marketing is unfocused and inconsistent. Without marketing, a brand never reaches the world at the right time and place. Similar to how a strong foundation keeps a building upright, branding sets up your marketing team for a successful return. And when your brand includes strong communication and design guidelines, it establishes a formula your marketing team can execute on. In other words, having a full complement of brand outputs will set you up for marketing success.

When you market your organization, product, or service before you establish a strong brand, you're leaving out the most important way to make an impactful and lasting impression on your audience—the only way to inspire a feeling that will keep them coming back.

Your brand should always influence marketing decisions. That's because your brand establishes what is important to convey to your audience, guides how to write copy that will draw people in, and figures out how to promote yourself in a way that stands apart from competitors and shows your audience that you are right for them. Let's go back to two questions I wrote above:

- Isn't branding just a marketing exercise?
- Shouldn't the marketing budget determine how much we allocate to a rebrand?

The answer to both is no. Hopefully, you can see why it would be foolish to limit the reach and budget of your rebranding efforts to a marketing effort alone. Branding is a top-line business effort that has a direct and powerful impact on marketing and growth. Our hope and motivation as an agency is that enthusiastic teams are able to rally all levels of their organization around how important the brand and marketing pairing really is—and how a successful rebrand can propel an entire organization forward.

Now that I've clarified the way that my agency views the meaning of brand and branding, how branding informs effective marketing, and how central branding is to any business as a whole, I want to approach the next two questions:

- When is the right time to consider a rebrand?
- How will you know that a rebrand is worth the costs and the effort?

Let's get into these in Chapter 2.

CHAPTER 2

WHEN TO REBRAND AND MEASURING ROI

Most companies encounter a collection of pain points and crossroads that prompt someone in the organization to ask, "Is it time to rebrand?" That could be a seed-stage company eager to define itself at the beginning of their journey, or a growing behemoth that's looking to reinvigorate through a rebrand. My goal in this section is to give you the confidence to understand if and when it's time to act.

Unfortunately, there is no yes/no beacon to signal that now is the time to act. However, there is a list of indicators that illuminate the right direction to take, and even when to take it. These indicators will answer both questions I posed at the end of Chapter 1:

- When is the right time to consider a rebrand?
- How will you know that a rebrand is worth the costs and effort?

Also, in the introduction I outlined the case for looking at branding as an investment. It is in that spirit that I add one more question to this list:

- Is now the time to invest in brand?

TIME TO INVEST IN BRAND

I've narrowed this list of indicators to the five most common ones that my agency has encountered since our inception. Combined, they account for roughly 95 percent of the brand engagements we tackle. As such, they've captured nearly all markets and client sizes and represent the most prevailing pain points and brand dilemmas our clients run into. If you're experiencing any of these indicators, you're reading the right book. If you see your organization experiencing one or more, it's definitely time to act.

1. YOU'VE REACHED AN INFLECTION POINT

This first indicator is the most common. True to its definition, an inflection point is a time of significant change—a turning point. Inflection points vary for every organization. Here are a few pivotal turning points that signal a clear YES to the question, "Is now the time to invest in brand?"

- The position of your organization is changing.
- Your organization is adopting a new name.
- A big culture shift is underway.
- Your brand architecture is broken.
- A significant merger or acquisition is taking place.
- There's been a major change to strategic vision.

- You're significantly diversifying your product or service stack.

These are a few very powerful, transformative moments in any business. Some happen because of successful business growth, while others occur at any time in an organization's life cycle. I'll say confidently that these instances can and should trigger brand action. I'll even argue that these moments are so fundamental and impactful to your organization that you cannot avoid a brand investment of some kind when they happen.

2. DUCT TAPE AND GLUE ARE HOLDING THINGS TOGETHER

Duct tape and glue is a close second in what we see and work through with clients. These situations arise when a brand prioritizes short-term thinking but sacrifices long-term goals. It focuses on making things work now versus making everything work better.

Maybe you began with brand clarity, but over time things became disheveled. It could be because your company dove right into product marketing and never resolved your brand in the first place. Or maybe it's been so long since you looked at your brand that it's impossible to tell what's official from what's not.

Every business travels a different path. But a patchwork application without a solid brand foundation leaves other staples of your business (marketing, product decisions, customer experience, company vision, etc.) stuck in a tiring game of whack-a-mole. Decisions become reactive and lack direction.

What should be energizing becomes exhausting. Here's how this plays out within an organization:

- Brand assets are severely limited at best. At worst, they're nonexistent.
- Teams create and implement assets based on departmental needs and guesswork rather than organizational strategy and direction.
- You never defined a clear messaging framework, and communications come across as random or speculative.

It's hard to capture momentum when duct tape and glue are holding your brand together. Your businesses cannot grow, evolve, or improve in this scenario. To your market, these indicators signal weakness. To customers, they muddy the picture of your organization. In the end, these indicators create distrust both externally and internally. Whether there ever was a brand strategy is beside the point because inconsistency has become the rule. If you are struggling with these issues, it is time to invest in brand.

3. YOUR BRAND EXECUTION LACKS CONSISTENCY

A lack of consistency is closely related to the duct-tape-and-glue scenario. While duct tape and glue is more about cobbling assets together based on in-the-moment needs, the lack of consistency points toward how you apply the assets you possess.

A discontinuous or non-existent brand presence creates a non-entity—a rudderless ship. Consistency builds loyalty, recognition, and trust; together, these lead to strong brand equity. Perhaps your vision, mission, and positioning are compelling, and you've created strong marketing outputs that reflect them. That's a big win! However, if your company's visuals and voice don't reflect these appropriately, you're undermining the work that led to your vision, mission, and positioning in the first place. Here are a few ways this scenario plays out within an organization:

- Your brand visuals clash with your brand voice (or vice versa).
- You're upholding your brand standards in your customer experience but not in your social media presence.
- Your website embraces your brand, but your office houses relics of an older brand iteration.
- Your vision presents a culture of A, but you operate as a culture of B.
- Marketing efforts apply your brand assets and messaging haphazardly.

A recent report from Marq, a brand templating platform, captured this point well with concrete data. I wish I could say the results are surprising:

- The upside of consistency: 68 percent of respondents reported that consistency in their brand execution contributed from 10 to more than a 20-percent increase in their revenue growth.
- Still, 31 percent said that they follow brand guidelines selectively.
- Meanwhile, 77 percent said that they witness off-brand content creation within their organization, with 22 percent of this happening monthly.[6]

---

6   Marq, 2021 *Brand Consistency Report*, 2021, https://pub.lucidpress.com/brand-consistency-report/.

Imagine a Disney World employee speaking in a snarky, unempathetic voice or Apple using a childish font on a random page within their website for no clear reason. Those inconsistencies damage brands and affect how the public perceives them, even if it's a small, one-off experience. Unfortunately, looking at the data above, you can see that these situations are rarely one-offs. The bottom line is that if a brand wants to be successful, it cannot afford inconsistency. Closing this gap—no matter how small—will pay for itself.

4. CONFUSION REIGNS

Confusion shows up like a culminating trickle-down effect from one or more of the three challenges above. Think about it: if you lack solid brand footing, if you're using duct tape and glue, or if you're inconsistent across brand touchpoints, what else would you expect but confusion? How can anyone—customers, partners, employees—know who you are or what you stand for when you're constantly saying something different, or nothing at all?

But here's an interesting thing about confusion: it can be a result of one or more of the pain points above and can also cause them. That's one of the main reasons I've included confusion as its own entry. It's not just a symptom; it can be an underlying factor. When it is a factor, it signifies an error in positioning, which is central to brand perception.

We run into aspects of confusion often with clients—situations where people see themselves as one thing but struggle to communicate it. Organizations with complex technical or product-centric offerings are even more susceptible to this pain point. Here are a few ways that confusion plays out within the organization:

- Your internal culture is either disconnected or contrary to how the organization represents itself, or how others view you.
- Your position in the market is unclear, which leaves customers passing you over, not realizing you may be the perfect fit for them.
- Your product is at the top of your industry, but your business is unable to grow market share.

If you haven't spent the time focusing on clarifying your position or identifying how your offering lines up with customers' needs, then you are letting the market write its own narrative. Outside voices will construct their own assumptions about how you may or may not benefit them. Your appeal will never go beyond the surface level, and no one will know the true value of your offering, culture, or mission.

5. YOU'VE SIMPLY GROWN UP

The first four indicators signal some brand problems that arise. This fifth indicator is different. It's a result of growth and maturity. Maybe your organization has reached a point where a rebrand will allow you to capture your true personality and aspirations. Perhaps some key decisions have panned out, and now you're experiencing accelerated growth in all the right places. Whatever the case may be, if your business is evolving but your brand is lagging behind, it's time to capture who you are and who you want to be by investing in your brand.

This pain point has extra relevance for me. Our agency had this exact realization shortly after we wrapped up our first decade in business. On the surface, we were doing just fine. Nothing was critically broken. Our customers loved working with us, our values were clear, and our processes were tight. However, even with the level of progress we'd achieved, we were suffering from some fallout from our growth. Here are a few ways this played out for us, and how it might play out for you:

- Our brand still represented our current self but not our future vision.
- Our position had become more and more focused, but we weren't conveying this evolution externally.
- Our visuals weren't bad, but they didn't capture the expertise we now championed with our clients.
- While our voice was still on-brand, our messaging didn't speak directly to our customers in the way we knew it could.

At the time, we definitely identified with the irony that exists in the parable of the cobbler and his kid: We were making awesome shoes for clients, but our own footwear needed some help. Perhaps you identify with a similar notion: your brand improves things for others but downplays the importance of doing the same for yourself. If you can look at yourself and see that you need new shoes, then it's time to invest in your brand.

One last note on this final pain point: When we realized that we needed to rebrand, we didn't throw out years of equity. Instead, we leaned into a number of highly valuable aspects of our organization as we iterated toward the future. This can be the case for you as well. Keeping the elements that make you special, like your beloved culture and values, are essential to the rebrand process. First, you must willingly invest in your brand. Once you do, you're staking claim to the future your growth has led you toward.

DON'T TAKE THE EASY WAY OUT

It's easy to address any of these challenges at the symptom level, which is why it's a common practice. Don't fall into that trap, or you'll wind up right back in a duct-tape-and-glue situation in a few weeks.

You have to address any of these challenges at their core, which is the brand level. Otherwise, they'll perpetuate, get worse, and erode any brand equity you possess. Then, in a hurry to right the ship, you'll wind up throwing money at new features or one-off campaigns to (hopefully) get people excited. Here's a scenario from a recent client engagement:

- **Presenting symptom:** The organization's voice didn't match the brand visuals across touchpoints; most notably their website.
- **The client's initial reaction (before working with Focus Lab):** Drum up some new language for the website.
- **The issue:** thinking they could write new communications for one touchpoint without considering how to make sure it aligned with their brand and all other touchpoints. They built new comms in a bubble to solve the website alone. They addressed the symptom but not the root issue.
- **Proper solution:** creating a larger communications framework tied to the core mission of the company, which the client deployed across all channels.
- **The result:** a brand that speaks like it looks, across all

channels, and a framework that can be built upon moving forward, reducing future friction. This clarity and consistency will create deeper trust internally and externally, resulting in an actual long-term impact, not a quick and dirty "fix."

Does it take longer to address a root issue? Yes. Doing so also leads to a longer, more profitable result.

THE COST OF DOING NOTHING

One of the biggest questions you can ask before you move forward with a rebrand is this: what is the cost of doing nothing? It doesn't matter why you're doing nothing—budget, fear, uncertainty, timing, etc. You can toss all of the reasons away and get down to more vital questions: What happens if you continue to stick with what you have? What will you be missing? Will your competition move ahead? Will the market pass you by?

Here are the actual costs of doing nothing. First, your business fails to realize its potential. Eventually, you become irrelevant in a saturated market. It sounds dramatic, but it's true.

Granted, for brands with deep equity or bottomless budgets, the cost of doing nothing can be less intense. They might decide to just keep reinforcing what they have and letting the existing story do its thing. But for most companies, the cost of doing nothing is complete and utter stagnation, which is fatal for a business. That's because when a brand fails to self-actualize, it leaves its audience and internal teams hanging in the balance.

Let's be straight here: your business wants to win, as does every business. In many cases, a strategic rebrand is the leap you need to make in order to accomplish this goal. Consider the following questions:

- Does your mission ring true?
- When customers experience your brand, do they only get a list of features and products in a silo?
- Do customers gain a deeper understanding of what your company stands for?
- How well do you appeal beyond the surface?
- Are customers buying what you do, or do they invest in the bigger reason that exists *behind* what you do?

If you only take one thing away from this chapter, this is the question I really want you to sit with in regards to your brand: what is the cost of doing nothing?

IS A REBRAND WORTH IT?

We've discussed indicators that say it's time to rebrand, along with the cost of doing nothing. Let's look at some questions that many clients ask when they're on the cusp of deciding to DO something about their brands:

- What is the actual return on brand investment?
- How will we know we've made the right decisions?
- Is this worth it?

These are very important and understandable questions, especially considering the size and implications of a rebrand. The truth is, measuring brand ROI can be hard to do. To try to answer these questions and help you have a better picture of the risk/reward scenario, I'd like to address them from a few different angles.

First, I'll highlight a very tangible example from a past client that has since gone on to its IPO. From there, I'll share a simple fact that not many people know but that brilliantly illustrates the potential in intangible assets. Then I'll bring things closer to home with some direct perspectives from former Focus Lab clients. Finally, I'll finish with a story highlighting a common thread.

ROI THROUGH CAPITAL RAISE AND IPO

Braze is a leading customer engagement platform. In 2016, after raising $20 million in Series C funding, they were ready to move forward from their previous name (Appboy), along with their startup look, feel, and messaging. They wanted to conquer the next steps in their company journey, and a rebrand was necessary to propel that vision and momentum. They very much fell into pain point number five from the list above (You've Simply Grown Up).

They worked with an agency called Lexicon on their new name, then hired us to create a brand that matched the power of their platform and clarity of their vision. After months of valuable collaboration, the new brand was born, now called Braze. With their new brand in hand, Braze had its public launch, and later that year, raised $80 million in Series E funding. That's a 300 percent increase in value over a single year.

Granted, I can't tie all of this success to their new brand, but for argument's sake, let's say the new brand had a 5 percent effect on their value. That equates to $3 million.

In 2021, Braze announced their IPO on the NASDAQ. They raised $520 million, hitting a new value of $8.4 billion. By now, that 5 percent effect from brand has compounded to $425 million. Again, I understand the product also needs to be superior, the leadership needs to be excellent, and the culture needs to be world class to achieve these milestones. But don't forget, the brand's job is to express each of those. If it fails, that will have a direct and negative impact. However, if it succeeds, it will create a positive effect, as was the case with Braze.

The bottom line: brand multiplies your successes and helps you identify opportunities to create more. Braze understood that investing in brand was an essential factor in helping achieve this level of success and capturing a hefty return on their brand investment.

ROI THROUGH MERGER AND ACQUISITION

As I wrote in the intro, for companies considering a potential merger or acquisition, a clear and solid brand can substantially impact valuation. Investors were surprised to see that 70 percent of the $13 billion acquisition price for Whole Foods was allocated to "goodwill," suggesting Amazon paid heavily for existing intangible assets and future potential.[7]

In fact, Amazon paid $9 billion beyond the tangible assets on Whole Foods' balance sheet. Take a minute to let that sink in. This isn't just an outlier involving a big name with big money. This happens all the time and will become more common in

---

7   Eugene Kim, "Amazon's Soaring Goodwill Balance Shows How Whole Foods Buy Was a Long-Term Bet," *CNBC*, February 6, 2018, https://www.cnbc.com/2018/02/06/amazon-10-billion-goodwill-balance-shows-whole-foods-strategy.html.

the future. In our market of B2B tech, acquisition term sheets often contain an explicit line item for brand. That line item is where a brand's value shows up in real dollars.

ROI IN VARIOUS FORMS

We all have different brand problems, definitions of success, and goals when we consider return on investment. Not every organization desires an IPO, or to get acquired. How do you measure ROI if not just in big numbers?

In the past few years, I've spent time speaking with clients post-rebrand to uncover these various returns, in their words. My goal with these interviews is to pull back the curtain on their rebrand experience so anyone considering a rebrand can get an authentic, unabridged perspective.

As part of each interview, I ask our clients to address the ROI they are experiencing. Here are a few genuine answers I've received, word for word.

Humberto Ayres Pereira, CEO, Rows

This rebrand effort has paid itself off in less than a year. It's one of the best investments I've made, ever, in being a part of a startup, and this is my fourth time. Early on, this rebrand saved us a ton of money in hiring fees. We were trying to hire fifty or more people over a few months. Having a better brand where everything agrees really makes it easier. We had an applicant reach out and tell us she saw the awesome rebrand, and from that moment on wanted to be a part of our company.

Marcus Olson, Founder, Pliancy

When I think about the ROI of our rebrand, it's probably 100x over the past five years. It's the best investment I've ever made. Everything stems from that. We provide better services than others because we hire the right people. The right people are attracted to our company because they witness our brand and understand what we are all about. How did we do that? We punched above our weight class and hired the best brand agency we could find. The ROI is immeasurable. Without the brand we wouldn't be where we are.

A FINAL STORY

Every now and then our Focus Lab team and I travel out to a client's headquarters to spend the day completing different discovery exercises. On one trip to Seattle, we had just completed an archetypes exercise and found ourselves on a short break. We were sitting around a giant oak table in a glass-walled conference room, enjoying some downtime. At one point, a member of the client's team asked, "Why does it seem that every company Focus Lab works with is wildly successful? They either secure new rounds of capital almost immediately or get acquired. What's in the water?"

Everyone waited for me to reveal the magic answer. I pondered for a moment, then said, "Honestly, I can't suggest that we're the secret ingredient in every successful partnership. It boils down to a commonality our clients share: a clear understanding and deep appreciation for brand. They recognized that if they get their brand right, they will have a big leg up in their journey."

This answer surprised everyone in the room. After all, it was kind of an easy question, almost as if I asked him to ask it. In that moment, I was able to help their team realize that even without a spreadsheet of data to prove cause and effect, the results were real. Even better, the company in the room with us was following the same steps.

Having said that, I do believe the team at Focus Lab is special. We amplify the powers our clients bring to the rebrand journey. In Chapter 3, I will break down how this happens and why you should look for similar traits in any agency you partner with on your brand or rebrand journey. For now, when you consider the question of ROI, remember that while "brand" may be intangible, its value is very, very real.

CHAPTER 3

FINDING YOUR AGENCY

What's at stake when you're picking the right agency partner for your rebrand? As you're starting to see, quite a lot. In fact, this decision is just as important as the decision to invest in your brand. Now that you know you're going to rebrand, you can turn your energy to selecting the right agency for you.

Among the most important things to remember is that you might need to reframe the way you think about the traditional vetting process and what you're measuring. In that way finding the right agency is similar to measuring a brand's value: the intangibles are as important as the tangibles.

Throughout this chapter, I'll help you target what matters and ignore what doesn't. Before I outline exactly what you should and shouldn't look for in a partner, let me share another important note on reframing your perspective: you don't need to find an agency that understands your market better than you do.

Instead, you need an agency that understands *you* better than you do. One that will reflect back to you what you present to the world, will highlight points of conflict in your brand, and will give you a forum for expressing the real you.

SIGNS OF A GREAT PARTNER

What should you measure when it comes to selecting an agency? They should strive to provide impeccable care for your experience across every step of the journey, which includes giving equal attention and focus to the craft (the work), the process (the order of operations), and the intangibles (the experience). Combined, these aspects build lasting trust—a fundamental piece in a collaborative rebrand process.

Still, how will you know? What are the signs that your agency will put enough emphasis on these details? To help answer these and other questions, I've broken things down into something I'll call the three Ps: portfolio, process, and people.

Circling back to the three Ps is a great way to check various boxes and questions that will come up while you're vetting potential agency partners. In practical terms, they allow you to understand why awards mean very little, while past client experiences mean everything.

They also shine a light on why to avoid agencies that seem eager to jump in blindly and "knock things out" without a clear process. And they make it clear that the quality of an agency's work is table stakes, while customer experience is the secret sauce. Since an agency's portfolio is the most accessible and tangible starting point, I'll start there.

1. A PORTFOLIO OF PROBLEM-SOLVING

It goes without saying that you want your agency to produce exceptional work (again, table stakes). With this in mind, an agency's portfolio should be an initial screen in your vetting process but not the final check box. It's possible that your process will start by scouring the internet for examples of brand work that inspire you. Whose work is everyone talking about? Which agencies have competitors used? What's the latest trend that gets you excited about how your brand could "look"?

People can get overly focused, even to the point of distraction, on finding what they believe their future brand should look like or falling in love with something in an agency's portfolio. Rather than looking for a solution you expect you need, it's better to take the time to assess how an agency has solved previous clients' problems through brand. Remember: people don't fall in love and keep coming back to the swoosh. They buy Nike because Nike fulfills a need and lives up to a promise.

Early in our branding engagements, we advise clients to set aside personal preferences in favor of thinking strategically about their brand, the future, and their customers. Look at any agency's portfolio similarly.

- You may love their edgy visual design, but does that look and feel also work for your audience and will it convince them to buy?
- Does their work show how they solved the brand problem at hand or how they achieved results?
- Does their portfolio show a range of styles, showing that they have the flexibility to design for a client and their audience rather than their own aesthetic?

- Do they have results or testimonials that illustrate how their work has generated real impact?

Earlier I wrote that awards mean very little. I'll come back to this because it *can* be helpful to see that an agency has received a few awards and worked with some respected names. This tells you that at least some part of their craft is successful. But they're not the most important. Nor is their portfolio.

Your takeaway here is that an agency's portfolio confirms that they meet the table stakes to be part of your selection process. Once you scan the portfolio, be sure to take a deeper look: read case studies, find out how they solved various brand problems their clients faced, and continue to gauge whether their portfolio represents the kind of intentional work that your brand needs.

2. A PROCESS WITH TWO PARTS

At the root of any successful rebrand is a proven process. This cannot be overstated. I believe that process should hold more weight in your selection than an agency's portfolio. For the record, I would never have said this back when we started our agency. Back then, my design background blinded me into believing that everything revolved around pixels. Thankfully, I've matured in my perspective.

And I'm not alone. During the post-project debriefs I mentioned in Chapter 2, clients often share that the single most important factor in hiring Focus Lab, and subsequently the single most important piece of advice they would give to another company at the cusp of a rebrand, is to focus on the process. This is a key piece to remember about an agency's process: it's more than just a method.

What do I mean? My agency and I like to think of it in terms of a baking analogy that illustrates how there are two very important pieces of a sound process. To start, imagine you're going to the most famous bakery in the world, one known for its one-of-a-kind cakes. Their famous pastry chef is giving a workshop where you can learn how to make these cakes for yourself. You can feel the excitement in the air. Plus you already know the pastry chef has an incredible reputation—you've tasted her cakes for yourself, and they do live up to the hype.

Something strange happens when the class starts and you realize you're in trouble. The chef is speaking too fast, slipping back and forth between different languages you don't understand. She assumes that everyone in the workshop possesses a basic understanding of baking. Therefore, she's not taking time to guide you through this new experience. She never stops by your workstation to ask if you're confused or to clarify various reasons behind different decisions. Why use oil instead of butter? What is Dutch-processed cocoa? Why extra baking powder? She just says what to do and expects you to follow.

Since you trust her (she's an expert, after all), you try to make the best of things. However, taste-wise, your cake is a far cry from what you expected. Plus it's leaning to one side and is about to fall off its stand. Worst of all, you have no real idea how or why things went so horribly wrong.

Do you see what happened here? What failed? It wasn't the recipe, the tangible ingredients, or the order in which you followed the recipe. It wasn't the equipment. The failure came from her inability to understand, communicate with, and educate her class.

This is the first part of the two-part process element: Your agency has to understand that while they know how to do the work, it's equally important that they are able to guide you through it. If the agency's process doesn't include things you and your team need in order to collaborate, then it doesn't matter how qualified they are or what their portfolio communicates. Their process is incomplete, and the work you create together will suffer.

In the baking example, you needed one-on-one instruction and education so you could understand the entire process along the way. This is exactly what you should expect from your agency. You'll want to understand the rationale behind an agency's work as you progress through your rebrand. This helps you confidently roll it out to your team and make educated decisions as you continue beyond the rebrand launch. Here are some questions to ask to find out if an agency can relate their process to you:

- Did they do a good job of explaining their expectations of your commitment?
- Did they lay their process out in a way that makes it easy for you to follow?
- Were they able to describe their work in a way that makes sense to you?
- Did they take time to listen to your concerns and expectations?
- Did they give you ample time to ask questions?

- Did they spend at least as much time learning about you as they did talking about themselves?
- Do you feel confident that they are people you can tackle challenges and challenging conversations with?
- Do you know who you will be interacting with, what their roles are, and when?
- Did you learn anything?

Now onto the second part of the equation: the method itself. As you are vetting agencies, here are a few questions to ask to help you understand how their process works:

- What does their process look and feel like?
- How will their process set up your team for success each week?
- How will you know where you are in the project week to week?
- What are the deliverables and when will you get them?
- Are there key milestones you should know about and prepare for?
- How should you involve larger stakeholders into the process without wrecking the timeline?
- What happens when someone gets sick or takes vacation?
- What tools will they use to communicate and interface with your team?
- Will you have a dedicated project manager on the project?

Every agency's process is different, which adds to the uncertainty when deciding whose is best. Remember the notion of "best" is something you measure by what works for you in terms of the work itself and the agency's ability to communicate that clearly.

As for clients that select our agency, we align to their needs for a repeatable, easy-to-understand process that puts them at the center. We produce and deliver work in a week-to-week, iterative cadence and meet with client teams on the same day every week throughout the duration of the rebrand. There is rarely, if ever, a moment when a client might think, "I wonder what Focus Lab is working on or when we are going to get it."

This has a huge impact on the general momentum, feel, and sense of trust that forms as a project continues. As a fully remote agency, we've always structured our process to balance asynchronous working periods with synchronous touchpoints. It's nice to be able to rely on a dose of consistency when you're in the midst of a monumental effort such as rebranding.

Here's another aspect that lands somewhere between process and people: how an agency positions the team that will be working on your project. Our agency places great value on our clients, their internal teams, and the individual roles they take on within a project. With this in mind, we place equal attention on how we position our own team members.

Some agencies give off a "walled gardens" vibe, where the project manager is their only touchpoint and the agency holds you at arm's length from the process and team members on the agency's side. Sadly, this approach creates silos and breeds discontent. In this scenario, clients feel like they're mere observers and that the project manager is the only one in control.

Our agency takes a much different approach. Our team members—the people doing the work—have direct and regular (weekly) contact with clients. We believe that these craftspeople are the right ones to speak to their work and answer questions related to it. Having done the research and produced the work, they have the rationale and understand the vision when it's time to explain things. The project manager will still be there, but they will act more like a shepherd than a messenger. We'll talk more about the project manager in Chapter 4. The point here is that you should find out what your relationship will look like in order to make the best decision for your team.

3. PEOPLE THAT CARE ABOUT PEOPLE

People have a critical place in a rebrand partnership. I've shared this already, but let me reiterate: A brand project is a partnership in every sense of the word. Two teams must come together to accomplish a shared goal, equally reliant on one another for success.

I'll refer back to Chapter 2's debrief client interviews. What our clients realize after having experienced a rebrand journey from start to finish is that the people piece is perhaps the most vital element of all. Here's one of many quotes I'd like to share:

"Through Focus Lab, we've discovered that brand is built around the heart and soul of the people that make up a business. It's not just what you are but why you are. It's like seeing a really good therapist. You talk it out. You are challenged, encouraged, inspired, and if you work the process, you'll come out on the other side with a better brand and with better people."

—TODD CALVERT, BRAND DIRECTOR, ZELLO

What does it mean to be a good partner? To borrow some of Todd's thoughts:

- A good partner pushes you to be your best.
- They leverage expertise and empathy throughout the rebrand journey.
- They're not driven by ego yet are comfortable sharing strong opinions. In fact, they never forget that opinions are a must!

A good rebrand partner also helps you see blindspots (helping you understand yourself better than you have before) but never believes that they are the only ones with great ideas. They are able to shepherd you through the process, like our baker from earlier should have done, even if it means having difficult conversations along the way.

How can you measure the people factor within an agency? There are two main pieces to consider here: personality fit and culture/values fit. Even though they often blend together, I've broken them out below to help unpack each one.

Personality Fit

It's worth seeing the value in a connection beyond just the words that people use. When you speak with members of the agency, does the conversation flow naturally and feel like you and they are speaking the same language? You don't need your agency to be a complete reflection of you. In fact, you wouldn't want this to be the case. But the connection—the personality fit—should feel natural nonetheless.

On the other hand, if it feels like you're two parties sitting on opposite sides of the table, unable to get to the same side, make note. If there's something missing in the connection, whether emotional or otherwise, that gap will amplify when big decisions arise mid project and conversations get challenging.

Short of taking personality tests, here are some questions you can ask to help gauge how well your personalities fit:

- Am I excited to work closely with these people for the duration of this long project?
- Did it feel like I was talking to a partner or to a vendor?
- Was it pulling teeth to keep the conversation going?
- Do I feel like they actually heard me or like they were just reciting a script?

I can't tell you the number of times that people say hiring us "just felt right." That feeling is driven by the right answers to the questions above. Obviously, you will have more to go on than just these answers, but you can't ignore a sense of connection—or lack thereof. Trust your gut in such moments.

Culture and Values Fit

Does the culture of the agency feel like one you could see yourself fitting into? Looking from the inside out, I can tell you it's easy for me to see many of our clients living within the culture at Focus Lab or vice versa.

A cultural fit is a strong supportive undercurrent to rely on during a rebrand. It brings individuals together in a way very similar to personality fit. Remember your agency is more than a vendor; they're an intimate partner in your brand transformation. When working to discover their culture and values, consider asking yourself the following:

- Do their company values align with ours? (Ask for examples of how they live up to or measure them.)
- Do they value transparency?
- Are they willing and able to answer tough questions?
- Did they seem to be interviewing you as well? (This is a great indicator they also care about culture/values fit.)

When the culture and values of the agency are clear, it won't be hard to determine the character of their organization and people.

Meeting the Team

You might wonder if you'll have the chance to meet "all the people" on the agency's team or think that you *need* to meet them. Let me assure you that you don't need to spend your efforts here. Yes, your point of contact might be a single person, particularly at a smaller agency. It might even be a founder. At a larger agency it's probably a dedicated sales or support team member. Don't assume that one is better than the other.

Can you measure the cultural fit after talking with just one person? I believe you can. If an agency has done a good job creating shared values and building a rock-solid culture, both will shine through in your contact. Yes, they should be able to clearly describe the team you will be working with, but it is not critical that you meet that team before you can decide whether that agency is right for you. (To note, at Focus Lab we rarely if ever pull team members away from current work so they can join a sales call. We'd rather protect their time and our clients' projects.)

If having only one point of contact feels risky, feel free to speak up. Remember that the main value you gain with additional touchpoints is to confirm that an agency's values and people factor permeate across their entire ecosystem. When a department director, project manager, or even a founder joins the call, if you get the same feeling from them as you'd gotten from your first point of contact, you can trust that the organization is walking in the same line.

The three Ps (portfolio, process, and people) will serve as a powerful guide in your agency search. They are so important within our agency that we've created an acronym for it and measure ourselves against it with every project. We call it SAUCE: seek to achieve unforgettable customer experiences. It's our promise to customers to value the intangible aspects of any project to the same degree we value the tangible.

As you consider agencies, consider whether they pay attention to the intangibles. They don't need an acronym, but they do need to show that they understand how much value the intangibles bring.

SPECIALIST VS. GENERALIST AGENCY MODELS

Now you have a sense of how and why to use the three Ps when selecting the right agency. As you continue through your vetting process, whether or not the agencies you're exploring have their own version of SAUCE, you will likely encounter two agency models: specialists and generalists. Here's a quick breakdown:

- Specialist agencies will be hyper-positioned in their service offering, communicating things like: "We do one thing and at a level others do not. We do it over and over successfully for people just like you."
- Generalist agencies will communicate a wide range of services and cover different verticals, sometimes seemingly at random, saying things like "We do everything you need, and we can make it seamless and your life easier as a result."

If you are lining up a short list that includes agencies from both camps, I advise you to choose a specialist, especially if you want the best results in terms of craft.

- With a specialist firm, you can capture the dedicated experience and complete focus of passionate experts who tirelessly address your pain points.
- Specialists in craft understand techniques in a way that allows them to capture nuance better than generalists do.

Before you trip over the idea that it will be harder to execute on your project if you need two vendors, a brand agency plus a web firm for example, here's a tip: Specialists have great partnerships with other specialists. If brand is your foremost need, a specialist agency will bring you the most value.

THE WRAP ON SELECTING YOUR AGENCY

Finding your agency is a giant decision. Hopefully, this chapter has lifted some of the weight and shifted things toward measurables. Lean into the questions I shared throughout this chapter related to an agency's portfolio, process, and people. If you find yourself drooling over a portfolio but their process doesn't align with your needs, get clear on where and why.

At Focus Lab, we've learned that bending the process too far in any direction can be risky. If an agency holds tight to their process, don't assume they're just being inflexible. Ask them why. It may come down to the fact that they want to give you the best chance to succeed and they have reasons for adhering to their process that may not be immediately clear to you. Either way, ask for transparency about it.

In the end, your agency is there to help your company climb the rebrand mountain. When all is said and done, it's your journey, and finding the right agency makes your ascent a valuable and enjoyable one.

Part 2 of this book will turn the focus to practical matters: clarifying expectations and setting you up for project success via your project manager and the onboarding experience. Before I take us there, a number of key takeaways from Part 1 follow.

PART 1 TAKEAWAYS

CHAPTER 1 TAKEAWAYS

Your brand is the entire ecosystem around your company that leads to a feeling or perception in the eyes or hearts of customers.

- On its own, your logo will never accurately express the true power of your company. Your brand relies on multiple elements to add layer after layer of resonance.
- Branding comes before marketing. It is about who you are, why you exist, what you aim to achieve, and more. Marketing is the practice of expressing your brand to the world.

CHAPTER 2 TAKEAWAYS

There are five indicators that it's time to invest in brand:

1. **You've reached an inflection point**, and your brand needs to evolve with you.

2. **Duct tape and glue are holding things together**, and your brand decisions are reactive and lack direction.
3. **Your brand execution lacks consistency**, and inconsistency is eroding your brand trust.
4. **Confusion reigns**, and who you think you are doesn't match up with who your audience thinks you are.
5. **You've simply grown up**, and your brand has fallen behind your business.

- The cost of doing nothing may be insignificant. But it also may mean that your business fails to realize its potential.
- Brand may be an intangible asset, but the value of brand is real and quantifiable, such as in Amazon's valuation and acquisition of Whole Foods.
- ROI may take various forms, but it's very real when it comes to brand investment.

CHAPTER 3 TAKEAWAYS

You don't need to find an agency that understands your market better than you do. You need an agency that understands *you* better than you do.

- Evaluate potential agencies against the three Ps:
  - **Portfolio:** Don't evaluate it based on whether you like their work. Evaluate it based on their ability to illustrate how their work solves brand problems.
  - **Process:** There's the actual branding process and the ability of the agency to relate their process to you, the client. Make sure your agency has both.

- **People:** For the best match, look to confirm whether the people are a personality fit and the agency overall aligns with yours in culture and values.
- If a rebrand is what you need, favor specialists rather than generalists.

PART 2

ONBOARDING & PROJECT MANAGEMENT

Chapter 4 starts into topics you'll encounter in the transition from pre-project to in-project, from the moment you've signed on with your agency until the project kicks off. This chapter also marks something of a transition in the book's tone. Going forward, I'll share more of an inside look into how Focus Lab works in order to give you deeper insights and explain many of the practices that are easily overlooked.

AFTER YOU SIGN ON WITH YOUR AGENCY

If you followed some of the advice I shared in Chapter 3, then you've chosen an agency that cares about the customer experience. If that's the case, then they also will have a clear onboarding process for you to follow.

To help you be most successful, even if your agency gives you a kickoff date weeks in the future, you should think about "onboarding" as the entire window of time between signing the contract and kicking off the project. You'll enter this phase with questions, and you'll have some work to do. If you've selected your agency well, they won't look at this period as being dead air. Instead, they will use this time to clarify expectations so that you know what you're getting into. Your agency should also seek information from you to help set their team up to hit the ground running.

This is the moment where the project manager (PM) will step up and take the reins. I'm going to put on my inner PM hat throughout this chapter and walk you through how the PM sets you up for success.

THE IMPORTANCE OF THE PM POSITION

Your agency's PM will clarify expectations for the project to come. Focus Lab, like many agencies, assigns a designated PM as a key part of your project team. In my view, the PM is a must have. This dedicated professional will be your go-to liaison from start to finish—someone you can count on to keep both teams aware of and accountable to the process.

The PM is an expert guide in the process. PMs know where you and the agency want to go, and possess the professional and personal skills to point out various routes and respond to pivots along the way. Like a lead mountain climber, PMs know what weather is coming and are not shy when it's time to regroup or rest. They are ready to walk the path with you.

At Focus Lab, PMs are more than just administrative go-tos. In fact, your PM is there for anything you want to talk about, big or small, tangible or intangible. Our agency's PMs are empowered to make decisions, adjust timelines, provide supportive guidance, and remain as quick as necessary on the draw.

PMs also have deep knowledge of the branding process and will weigh in if they see something on either side that needs attention. They run point and keep everyone focused and aligned. We value PMs so highly for the continuity they bring to a team during a big rebrand that we highly recommend our clients add a PM on their side as well. I'll come back to this point later in this chapter and again in Chapter 5 when I discuss the ins and outs of building your internal project team.

ONBOARDING

I can vividly remember one specific kickoff call during our second year in business. We were a team of five back then, still figuring it all out. Huddled tightly over an Ikea desk in a tiny co-working office in downtown Savannah, my business partner, Erik Reagan, and I dialed into a conference call. This client set a new bar for us—they were our biggest client to date—and the excitement was high. This call would be all about outlining expectations for the first few weeks of their rebrand.

Here's the thing: we didn't have a clear onboarding process back then. We were confident that we could simply chat through expectations and answer questions. After all, we'd been doing this for two years by now, relying on our ability to lead an organic but often random assortment of topics while outlining various expectations as we moved forward in a project.

When the call ended, the client was happy, but Erik and I agreed that we had to do better moving forward. From that moment on, we've never disregarded the importance of having a clear and thorough onboarding process. It's something we continue to iterate on after all these years.

Project onboarding is such a critical step in the rebrand process—much more than a simple meet-and-greet call. It sets the tone for everything that follows and helps you acclimate to the details and nuances of a branding experience with confidence. The onboarding experience answers many questions, including:

- What do I need to get started?
- What do they need to get started?
- How will the project flow?
- How do I access project information?
- Who will I be communicating with and how?

Even if you feel like you received these and other answers during the sales process, keep in mind that the rest of your team did not. The onboarding experience shares these same expectations with other members of your project team so everyone is on the same page.

By the time the onboarding phase wraps up, you should have a clear understanding of what your agency expects and needs from you at different stops along the way. Most importantly, you should feel confident that you are on the path to rebrand success. Here are a number of valuable pieces within the onboarding process:

SALES-TO-PM HANDOFF

As I mentioned, at the start of your onboarding you'll meet with your PM, who will serve as your go-to point person on everything. At Focus Lab, we make this introduction in what we call our "sales-to-PM handoff," a dedicated meeting with the sales point person, the PM, and the client-side pointperson to ensure the experience is fluid.

This meeting (whether virtual or in person) walks you through the steps that will come next, doubles down on the agreed-upon scope, and addresses any nuances and pre-project questions one last time. It's a chance to get ahead of potential disruptions like vacations, conferences, new team members, or anything else that might jostle the team or the timeline. This meeting is also a chance to discuss your responsibilities, including the very important ins and outs of building your project team (more on that later).

A PEEK AT THE DRIVER ROLE

In many cases, the person who engages with the agency on the sales side continues to be the project owner, or "driver" per the DACI framework, for the duration. I'll define the driver role in detail in Chapter 5, but I want to offer a quick peek at this role now. Since you're the one reading this book, you may wind up being the driver on your team.

From an agency's perspective, having an empowered and accountable project driver is critical to the success of a rebrand project. From sales to onboarding through launch, the information and expectations that drivers share during the sales process and the responsibilities they hold must stay consistent and must not get lost.

Even though you might wind up being the driver for your team, there are plenty of cases where the person who seeks and signs the contract does not have the bandwidth to be the driver or isn't sure they are the right person for the job. Again, more on this to come in Chapter 5. The key takeaway here is a driver will be defined in the onboarding process.

TOOLS

During the handoff meeting, you and your agency will discuss the various tools you'll be using to collaborate, so you should gain a clear picture of what you'll use for:

- Deliverables
- Synchronous communication (i.e. scheduled meetings)
- Asynchronous communication (i.e. agile situations)
- Calendaring
- Project scheduling
- File sharing and management

No matter what tool your agency uses as their communication hub, make sure that you have access to it, and expect your dedicated PM to bring you into the fold during your project onboarding. Keep in mind you may have to learn a new tool in order to work most effectively with the broader team. If the tool your agency uses is new to you and you're worried about the learning curve, speak up early.

SYNCHRONOUS COMMUNICATION

Make sure you understand what your synchronous, live touch-points will be and whether they work for you and your team. Focus Lab schedules these meetings with clients during the onboarding process. These meetings keep us connected, give us space to discuss the week before and the week ahead, and continue building team rapport.

ASYNCHRONOUS (OFFLINE) COMMUNICATION

It's important for any agency to designate a communication channel for offline communication—ideally something other than a slog of emails. At Focus Lab, we send anything written or visual through a single channel. This keeps all communication centralized, makes sure that everyone on the project has access to the complete log of communication, and ensures that you always know where to go if you need to reach someone outside of the project's regularly scheduled meetings.

YOUR RESPONSIBILITIES

The start of onboarding is the moment when you will come up to speed on the things you and your team will need to do before kickoff. Below I've listed a number of steps as something of an easy-to-reference checklist of responsibilities for your project driver.

This list that follows may seem simple, but don't let its simplicity fool you into taking these responsibilities lightly. It's more of a cheat sheet of how to be the best client you can be. If you give attention to these tasks, your job as the driver will be easier, your project team and stakeholders will be happier, and your brand project will be as rewarding as it can possibly be.

1. BUILD YOUR PROJECT TEAM

I've mentioned your project team a few times by now. What I mean is a lean (ideally, four people, max), nimble, empowered task force of people who will meet with your agency and review and approve deliverables each week.

These people should receive dedicated time budgets to spend on your rebrand. They are knowledgeable about where your brand has been and where it needs to go. For them, this project is a priority, never an afterthought. They will need to have the capacity to spend several hours on the brand project each week. Building your project team is so important, I've made it its own chapter (Chapter 5). One important takeaway for now, though, is that this team should have both reserved time for the project and the authority to make brand decisions on a weekly basis.

Creating a well-represented team will ensure that you're empowered to make decisions, have captured valuable perspectives from inside your organization, and have the talents and voices you need to share responsibilities and champion the rebrand internally when rollout arrives. (I'll write more about the rollout in Chapter 10. I want to mention it here because it should be part of your early planning.)

Selecting the right team deserves spending time to get it right. Depending on your internal culture and team dynamics, it might be a real challenge, and you deserve as much guidance and time to sort it out as possible. This step is so important that

I'm going to come back to it shortly with a thorough "how-to" section that follows.

2. COMPLETE PROJECT PREP

Now that you've met the PM, gotten the lowdown on tools, and started to think about building your team, be prepared for your agency partner to give you project preparation work.

Either right before or after the handoff meeting, your PM will begin triggering a series of steps that will continue your immersion into the project. For some agencies, including ours, this includes some prep items for you to complete—the first set of actual work that will fall directly on you and your team.

You know your company and customers better than your agency ever will. Pre-project prep work is where you begin to transfer your knowledge over to your agency. It's different from just sending over existing brand materials or white papers. Remember your brand is at an inflection point. This preparatory material is meant to help your agency understand where you're going in light of where you've been and why. In the Focus Lab sphere, the purpose of this work and documentation is twofold:

- To gather deeper insights into your company so that we can prepare to meet with you with greater perspective.
- To allow us to make the best use of our time with you in the kickoff meeting.

For maximum clarity, here are a few of the assignments we ask customers to complete:

- **Audience breakout:** This spreadsheet captures and helps you characterize your target audience groups. The insights we gain help us understand your audience and market so that we can develop a brand that resonates with them.
- **Brand attributes exercise:** This is a collaborative exercise that helps you identify your future brand's attributes—how you wish to be perceived by your audience. We use these attributes as a litmus test for all the visual and verbal brand work to come.
- **Questionnaires:** We use questionnaires to gather deeper, open-ended insights into your business and brand needs. What are your current purpose, mission, and vision statements? Are they working for you? Who are your direct competitors? What are your growth goals? Learning more about the big picture of your brand situation helps us develop understanding early so that we can engage with you meaningfully from day one.

The biggest value in completing the preparation work will be to fuel the discovery period that began on the agency side as soon as you signed your contract. It's full of deep knowledge sharing and collaboration between our team and yours. (I'll share more on discovery throughout Chapter 5.) Here are a few other points to consider when preparing for the project prep work:

- I mentioned building your project team before you start your prep work. If you've built your team by now, or even if you have a good idea but haven't formalized your team, you can lean on these professionals to help you complete this work and to kickstart the continuity needed to make sure you all agree with the information you're providing.
- While it can be tempting to crowdsource input from as many

sources as possible, that can lead to disparate responses across prep items. I recommend that you choose only a few select people to help complete this work and that those people are your likely core project team members.

- Similarly, leverage the specific talents of the team members on your side to support in this preparation work. Let your head of customers fill out the audience breakout sheet, for example. Put the right people on the right tasks, then review everything before you bundle and ship it back to the agency.

The preparation work can be time consuming. It might be the first time you've articulated the situation that led you to engaging in a branding project. It might also raise questions that require you to gather other insights to answer.

Your agency PM will help set you up for success by sending this work out as far in advance of kickoff as possible and by helping you understand the time it requires so that you can carve out the time and resources to complete it.

From Focus Lab's perspective, the more thorough your effort is in completing your prep work, the better we can answer your questions and lead conversations on the topics that matter to you and your brand. We need your dedication even at this early point so that you get the most out of our efforts and focus. No matter how challenging the prep work is for you and your team, know that you will see a return on that effort. It's your first real opportunity to unload your brand burden onto someone who can help.

3. PLAN YOUR WEEKS

One of the biggest misperceptions I see from clients is an underappreciation for just how much time a rebrand project will take. Or a misalignment in how much time you expect to spend when compared with how much input you expect to have.

Let's say you've hired Focus Lab. In the end, we're going to do the lion's share of the work. However, since this is a collaborative process, you will have lots of contact with us. Yes, we will be producing and delivering the work, but you will have parallel responsibilities of your own. I'll break some of these down so you can see how things play out in practice during the project. I'll also add some words of advice and planning that we share with our clients.

First, though, let me define "deliverable," since it's going to show up a lot throughout the rest of this book. Deliverable refers to a specific item of work that we send to you for review. Deliverables can take many forms, including:

- A strategy document that outlines the proposed direction for the project.
- A communications doc that recommends a new value proposition.
- A design file that showcases the latest round of work on color and typography.

Essentially, anything you receive from your agency within the project scope is a deliverable. And believe me, you are going to receive a lot of deliverables. On Focus Lab projects, we ship at least one deliverable a week for the lifecycle of a project.

Depending on your role and the size of the project, the amount of time required to review each of these will vary. Below I've included some general (minimum) time expectations, using our own process as a model:

- Weekly project meetings with your agency to discuss feedback on deliverables and to plan for the week ahead. (1 hr. per week).
- Weekly check-in meetings between the agency's PM and the project driver on your side. (30 mins. per week).
- Time for your internal project team members to meet, review the latest set of deliverables, and consolidate feedback (more on this below). (2 hrs. per week).
- Time for your project driver to relay all of your feedback, using the agency's preferred communications hub. (30 mins. per week).
- Additional ad hoc meetings to discuss issues or topics as they come up (typically the agency's PM and your project driver). (30 mins. per week)

From this list, you can see that a rebrand is not a set-it-and-forget-it situation. It is a real project that is best served by having regular, predictable meetings with dedicated time and people. The time commitment can easily add up to at least four hours a week or more for everyone on your internal team. For your driver, the time commitment will most likely be more.

Knowing this, put these time commitments on your team's calendars. By understanding this focus on time early, you can plan for it before you begin.

In Chapter 10, I'll talk about additional planning considerations that will help you prepare for rollout and launch. For now, just know that your team and your planning should take into account both these project-specific considerations and post-project activities that support rolling out your new brand.

4. PLAN INTERNAL REVIEWS

As you just learned, internal reviews are a required touchpoint for your team. They help you gather clear opinions from each member of your project team and deliver these opinions in as thoughtful and intentional a manner as possible.

You might wonder why you can't just review every deliverable "live" with your agency and share feedback in the moment. Believe me when I say that doing so can be a mess. You and your team need time to process and discuss each deliverable on your own. That way, you're sharing thoughtful feedback with your agency rather than gut reactions.

There's another piece to this as well, and it's something that lots of agencies don't want to talk about: You are not going to love everything your agency delivers. It's a fact. That doesn't mean you won't eventually land on a fantastic solution. It does mean, however, that you won't love everything at first sight.

With this in mind, it's important to take time to review each deliverable, huddle with your project team, and hash out what's working and what's not. That is how you build valuable feedback and push toward a great outcome.

On the other hand, sometimes, you will love something immediately. However, if you build your internal team the right way, there will always be that one person who will offer a constructive contrarian perspective that helps you see things differently.

In both cases (not loving something or loving something right away), having time to review things as a team helps you build consensus before you provide valuable feedback to your agency.

Which leads me to the next point: What does "valuable feedback" actually look like from an agency's perspective? How is it structured? How will you know if you've covered what they need from you?

5. UNDERSTAND GOOD FEEDBACK VS. BAD FEEDBACK

Where communication is concerned, your largest responsibility comes down to how you communicate feedback after you review each deliverable. There is a lot to unpack in the word feedback, and it's important to be clear on how to navigate the time demands of each feedback cycle and the way in which to present feedback, beyond tools. While the onboarding phase doesn't include much in the way of feedback, now is a good time to review some feedback pointers that we share with our clients.

Be Honest

More than anything, be open with your thoughts and keep things real during your project. The sooner you adopt this philosophy, the quicker you and your agency will align and gain traction. Great feedback isn't littered with smile emojis and exclamation points. It's clear and it's honest. The phrase, "I hope I don't offend them" is a common mental trap. Yes, it's a thoughtful way to approach life, but it's counterproductive to the success of your rebrand.

If you've hired the right agency, you will very likely enjoy their company and have no malicious intent or interest in hurting their feelings. In the end, your rebrand process isn't about making people happy. Nor is it about raging at someone if you don't like the work. Honest feedback stays objective and focuses on the deliverable. It's respectful, clear, and conveyed in a way that moves the process closer to a successful outcome.

You will no doubt have moments where things feel very direct. This is a good thing. I promise you that your agency wants to know how you really feel. Guess what they don't want: to think that you're happy, only to find out later that you're not. When concerns come up, don't wait to share them.

Provide Critique, not Opinion

It can be difficult to separate personal preferences from functional, objective judgment. Knowing the difference goes a long way toward separating opinion from true critique. Here are some simple ways to do this:

- When reviewing a deliverable, don't ask yourself whether something is "good" or whether you "like it." Instead, ask whether it is successful. If you're not sure how to define success in this way, revisit each deliverable's stated goals and consider whether the work hits the mark.
- Remember: you and your internal review team are not the audience—your customers are. With this in mind, ask your-

self whether or not the work is appropriate for them. Look for indicators of success as it relates to the project and its goals, not a deliverable's personal appeal.

- Make your feedback actionable. While your agency wants to hear how you feel, what they really need is actionable feedback. For instance, they want to know that you don't like something because it doesn't achieve a stated goal. To deliver this type of feedback, articulate the things that aren't working. Is a certain aspect of it wrong? Does the piece create an effect that's the opposite of what you think it should be? Give your agency something to work with. Here's an example: rather than say something general like "this doesn't work," give something tangible like "this feels too playful for our audience."

Consolidate Feedback into a Single Voice

Consolidating feedback means gathering the collective feedback from your internal project team, forming and agreeing on a group consensus, and presenting your overall feedback as a single voice that asserts a clear position and directions. This task should be owned by your driver.

Having a single voice is key. One reason to really dedicate yourself to providing feedback in a single voice is because the alternative means giving your agency four different opinions on one input point and putting the onus on them to figure out which feedback is the most important or valuable, which isn't the best use of their time. This doesn't mean that you can't use your agency to reach consensus; you can. It means that in order to provide actionable feedback, your team needs to take the time to understand all input and perspectives before delivering them to your agency with any points of consensus and any points of disagreement clearly articulated.

The multiple-voices scenario can also create an unclear decision-making hierarchy. It might also stem from one. If you have four different sets of input, it adds implicit pressure on WHO is saying WHAT, which can lead the team to favor feedback from the person with the most organizational seniority rather than the person with the most insightful feedback. Not delivering single-voice feedback also means that your agency will spend the next full-team meeting talking through different opinions and hashing out the differences before anyone can move forward.

Consolidating feedback into a single voice gives you and your team members a chance to revisit and debate your own reactions to deliverables and make sure that everyone is aligned. These moments can serve as reminders of just how invested you are as a group to the success of your rebrand and the future of your company.

THE WRAP ON ONBOARDING AND PROJECT MANAGEMENT

Your onboarding experience, if done right, will give you a high level of confidence and structure to carry you through your rebrand journey. Doing this ahead of time frees you up to dedicate the majority of your focus on the work itself.

As your relationship with your agency PM grows, you'll see just how powerful this touchpoint really is, serving as a powerful bridge between you and your agency. Your PM is both a shepherd, supporting you through the unknowns of a rebrand as the agency voice, and an ambassador, representing your thoughts, fears, and victories inward to the agency team.

Understanding your time constraints and responsibilities and being clear in your planning and expectations will make a world of difference in your stress level and the quality of the collaboration. Ask your agency PM for best practices on this. And remember to look at this time as the necessary groundwork for giving you the tools and knowledge to ensure a smooth project.

Now that you have a better understanding of what will be expected of your team before and during the project and you have a liaison via your agency PM, it's time to delve into a topic I've mentioned several times: building your internal project team. Not all agencies will spend time on this topic, but at Focus Lab we've learned that in order to be the best agency we can be, we have to put ourselves in our customers' shoes and take the time to share what we've learned and give you some best practices for this important and often hurried task.

CHAPTER 5

BUILDING YOUR INTERNAL PROJECT TEAM

Selecting your internal project team can be a delicate, even contentious topic. A good team can make or break your project, so we're including our recommendations as well as resources you can use in case you have to communicate or explain what team choices you're making and why. As you read, if you get concerned about buy-in for these decisions, hang tight—I'll address different concerns as I go.

Even if you think you know exactly who you want on your project team, this chapter shares insights from the agency side that you will likely find informative. Whether or not your agency consults with you on how to build your team, we suggest keeping in mind the recommendations that follow.

Without being overly prescriptive, here are a number of parameters we share with our clients to help them build strong teams.

THE INS AND OUTS OF YOUR PROJECT TEAM

To start, "project team" is actually too simple a phrase for the team you're building. What you want is a super team of power players, filled with people who are willing to speak up when they spot something amiss, collaborate, and commit to seeing your rebrand through to its very exciting and transformative end. Where to start?

TEAM SIZE

The size of your internal project team matters. While project teams are going to vary in many ways, one trap we see is the idea that having more people is better. Trust me—having many voices doesn't equate to getting the right feedback or direction. More voices at a table, without clear roles and responsibilities, can make it difficult to reconcile differences, assign decision-making authority, and move forward as a group.

The problem is, keeping your project team tight can get tricky. You might find yourself in a situation where everyone wants to be on your internal project team, or where you think you need someone from each discipline within your organization. You might also be in a situation where company leaders want certain people to be in the room. Team size can balloon fast.

If your initial "short list" adds up to eight or nine people, you're still thinking too big. Instead, the nimbler your core team is, the easier it will be to stay focused, available, and effective. Our agency has found that the sweet spot for successful project teams totals three to four, but absolutely no more than five (and even with five some structure needs to be established). With this in mind, if you find yourself unsure of who to add—or subtract—start with these basic requirements:

- Remember those four hours per week I mentioned in the previous chapter? Who has time to be in weekly meetings, review deliverables in detail, follow up on tasks, do the prep work, galvanize other people, and get internal buy-in and approvals when needed? Each core team member must commit to this same level of time and involvement.
- Who has broad but functional knowledge of the challenge at hand?
- Who possesses or can assume authority and confidence to make decisions independently but enough humility to know when they don't know something?

ACCOUNTABILITY STRUCTURES

Individual responsibility and accountability are built-in expectations at Focus Lab. Accountability structures tell us who makes which decisions. Our agency works best with organizations like ours where accountability structures are clear and team members adhere to them. I want to be blunt about this topic because accountability—or lack thereof—can make or break your internal team.

If an organization lacks trust internally or leadership doesn't trust project team members to make decisions for which they are accountable, then throwing more people at a problem is not going to improve the work. Successful client teams assign clear roles and areas of accountability, delegation, reporting—a DACI model, with a driver, approver, contributor, and an informed role. Knowing and identifying this type of model gives team members a better chance to know their roles, responsibilities, and expectations at different turns.

PROJECT LEAD (DRIVER)

I mentioned the driver in Chapter 4. As the early champion of this effort, you may or may not be the person who leads the project going forward. No matter how things line up, the driver is the project lead. This person is literally "in the driver's seat." Your driver runs point for every interaction with your brand agency for the duration of the project.

Your driver is also responsible for managing your internal project team. This includes consolidating feedback into a single voice, which I stressed in Chapter 4. Most successful drivers know how to strike the balance between being highly organized and extremely tactful—someone who appreciates process and people. The driver aligns with the title Driver in the DACI framework. Here are some personal and professional attributes that drivers tend to possess:

- Your driver should be detail oriented, diplomatic, self-aware, and aware of others.
- Drivers usually possess specific knowledge of various aspects of the business and have the time and tenacity to close out their week-to-week tasks on time.
- Drivers are also capable of coordinating internal communication about the brand project to other members of the organization. This could be a big responsibility depending

on your org and decision-making structure and internal culture (e.g., if you have to get certain things approved by a non core team third party but that third party hasn't seen all the work to date, you will have to repackage the work in such a way that it stands a chance of success when presented to them.)

- Drivers have the time in their schedule to drive and to keep others on the road.

Again, whether or not you take the driver's role, ask yourself this: Do you want to be the person who consolidates all feedback and communicates with your agency's PM? Do you have the skills, attitude, personality traits, and professional acumen to nail this role? Can you move a team toward decision-making?

You might also be inclined to name the highest role on the org chart of your project team as your driver—the CEO or founder, for example. Before you do, the same question applies: does this person have the capacity to do all that is required while also managing his or her regular work tasks? In my experience, the answer is no. To select the right driver, focus on the traits, subject matter experience, and questions I've shared above, and don't worry about someone's title or place in the org chart.

THE DECIDER

The decider is empowered with authority to make decisions on behalf of the brand and is accountable for every decision during this process. Your decider aligns with Approver in the DACI framework.

- Regardless of company size or accountability structure, the decider must be present at weekly meetings and be able to make the majority of decisions on a weekly (or even daily) basis.

- In larger organizations with complex accountability structures, the decider might need to navigate and negotiate additional approvals with stakeholders from outside the core project team. If this is the case, then the decider has the additional responsibility of championing the work in order to get necessary approvals, which can be a very sophisticated interaction. Choose the person who might have this responsibility wisely.
- In some projects, the decider and the driver are the same person, but that's not always the case. In fact, it can be a good idea to split these two critical roles among different people, provided that the people in these roles complement each other and work effectively together.

Similar to the driver, the decider does not need to hold a senior-most position on the org chart. Most importantly, the decider must be able to resolve conflicts among internal team members and help people finalize decisions when they're on the fence. An ideal decider is pragmatic and shrewd but also empathetic—a good listener who is confident in his or her convictions and final decisions.

Since you're reading this book, you'll likely step into either the driver or the decider role. You might be better off handing the driver role to someone you trust to fulfill those responsibilities while you take the decider slot.

OTHER KEY CONTRIBUTORS

Now that you know how many people to target and which project-related roles you'll need to fill, let's focus on having the right people in some remaining seats. In a DACI model, these are your Contributors.

At the risk of being obvious, you want to gain insights from a cross section of organizational perspectives. The most common trap I see is assuming that you should stack your project team with people from your marketing department. I recommend taking a different approach because if your project team becomes too insular, it can result in groupthink, cause blind spots, and ultimately lead to failure to capitalize on your investment.

Sticking with the idea of keeping your team as nimble as possible, Focus Lab recommends filling out the remaining seats on your three-to-five person team with people from or with critical knowledge of the following disciplines, in order of relevance:

Marketing

If you're the CMO or VP of marketing, then the marketing wing of your project team is already covered by you. If you decide to add another marketing voice, lean toward someone who deeply understands your brand and has a good ear for how things need to shift. If your project includes significant communications (verbal identity) components for example, you'll want this person to bring that understanding to the table. And while this person may not be customer facing, it will be helpful for them to bring audience insights to the table.

Design or Product

Often a product manager, designer, solutions specialist, or creative director, this is someone who has a deep understanding of your product or service both now and in the future. Very importantly, this person should also understand the current gaps in your business and how the rebrand will help to fill those through the lens of their role.

Customer Experience or Customer Success

Whether someone comes from sales, customer service, or another customer-facing area of your business, this person should have on-the-ground knowledge of issues your customers and target audiences face. Having the voice of your customers in your ear during a rebrand effort is critical. Their perspective helps you and your agency identify mismatches that exist between what you offer and their perception of your offering. They also fill you in on the needs your customers face, of which you may only partially fill right now. Speaking from our agency's perspective, your customers show us how to appeal to your audience, what resonates with them, and much more. (A side note here: if your project team is becoming too big, we can source your customers' perspectives asynchronously.)

If you find yourself in a situation where you must choose between a second marketing representative and a customer success role, choose the customer role every time. Remember you are building a brand, not an email blast. You need the folks that will help you get to the root of your brand before you can communicate it to the world.

BUILD YOUR STAKEHOLDER NETWORK

By now, you are probably well on your way to building a full core project team. This section will help you flesh out additional stakeholders whose input or approval you might need. And if you haven't finalized your core project team just yet, you can also use this section to help figure out which role representations might be best. But don't take this section to mean that you must have a secondary set of stakeholders. In many cases, while adding this layer may seem critical at the outset, it actually adds complexity that gets in the way of your core project team. Think critically about what level of complexity you can sustain and whether you really need stakeholder touchpoints outside the core team or whether those are more of a nice to have.

For just about any type of project, it's critical to understand who may be interested in supporting your efforts as well whose input you might need at various points along the way. In a DACI model, these people are known as the Informed.

Your stakeholder network is also a way to include people who had wanted to be on your core project team but who didn't make the cut for one reason or another. Again, these are folks who may want to stay informed about the project but who don't need to be involved in the decisions or approvals.

This is also an opportunity to determine whether your decider will be able to make all necessary decisions or if you will need to gain approvals from people outside of your core project team. This could include people from executive leadership, key investors, board members, etc. The people in these roles may not be present during weekly project team meetings, but you may need their final approval before you can sign off on a deliverable or direction.

If there's someone out there whose input or approval you think you'll want or need during your rebrand or who will be instrumental in helping you build a team of brand advocates by keeping them informed of the project, add them to your stakeholder network. Here are a few subject matter areas to consider when you're building your stakeholder network:

TECHNOLOGY

For larger projects, or for those with a strong product component, consider gathering perspectives from people who understand what your company builds and delivers at a granular level.

FINANCE

Also for a larger project or one that involves a significant diversification of, or impact to, revenue streams, consider including a member of finance or someone who knows where and how the money comes and goes.

EXECUTIVE

CEOs like to be involved in rebrands but generally at a high level. Unless your company is very small, we recommend that you include the CEO as either a Contributor or an Informed individual (in the DACI framework) but not as an approver since they likely won't have the time for the weekly demands of that role. The CEO's input can be extremely informative from a business, brand, and vision perspective. They will certainly be invested in the outcome and will expect that someone from among key contributors will keep them informed during the process. Depending on your organization's size and style of operations, you may even seek executive input and approval at key moments.

BUILD YOUR INTERNAL COMMUNICATIONS PLAN

Now that you have your groups settled (project team and stakeholder network), it's a good time to begin building your internal communications plan. Here are some key points to consider related to how and when to communicate:

- First, share the recommendations I've offered throughout this section related to building an effective project team, including the team's size and composition. Keeping your broader network in the loop will help ensure that you have support in your efforts and that no one is caught off guard when they don't see their name on your project team list.
- If you have a fully empowered decider, communicate to your larger network that decisions will run through them rather than needing executive or other level approval.
- In addition, outline and share your plans for keeping your extended stakeholder network educated and informed as the project goes on. A solid internal communications plan can help bring people along with you in your efforts and affirm the autonomy of your project team.
- As part of your communications plan, list names and roles of people who hold various levels of decision-making authority.
- Share your expectations for executive stakeholders and their involvement in the project.
- Decide on what level of communication you plan to share related to the project's progress and how often you want to update non-project team members and contributing stakeholders.

- Finally, if anyone has veto power at any level, account for this within your communication plan and let your agency PM know about this and where any touchpoints with that person may be.

In terms of timing, take this early opportunity to practice communicating about the project and getting internal buy-in, even if you have to baby step it. In fact, start right after the PM hand-off meeting I wrote about in Chapter 4. Don't wait until you are a few weeks away from launching your new brand to start communicating about it or going to executives for approval. I'll come back to this thought when I discuss key deliverables starting in Chapter 6.

Above all else, you want to bring your team along with you in your crusade. To do so, you will need to guide them, with help from your agency, in the direction that is best for the future of your company. When you lead with confidence and clarity, they will follow with enthusiasm and become ambassadors for your brand.

THE WRAP ON BUILDING YOUR INTERNAL PROJECT TEAM

Your newly formed core project team will lead the charge on this rebrand, bringing their diverse perspectives and sharing responsibilities to make for a successful outcome. Taking the time and energy to bring together the right team and the right communications plan will pay off from week one when you realize you have clear roles and responsibilities, everyone is there for a reason, and you can focus on the work rather than being distracted by disorganization. Even if the agency you partner with doesn't talk you through this step, I hope you will take a cue from these recommendations so that you can build the most effective project team possible.

We're nearing the halfway point of the book and are about to dive deep into strategy, discovery, comms and design. Before we get there, I'd like to share key takeaways from Part 2's focus on onboarding, project management, and building your internal team.

PART 2 TAKEAWAYS

CHAPTER 4 TAKEAWAYS

Even if your kickoff date is weeks away, "onboarding" begins as soon as you sign your contract.

- Enter this phase with questions.
- Be prepared to do some work.
- Clarify your expectations so you know what you've signed up for.
- Be a good partner for your agency when they ask for information and input—it helps them do their job.
- Don't be afraid to reach out to your agency at any point during this phase.

Your agency's PM is about to take the reins. Here is an expectation for your project manager and the onboarding experience:

- Get to know and build rapport with your agency's dedicated PM. They will be your go-to liaison for weeks to come.

Onboarding is also a time to start gathering a number of key pieces to fit the overall puzzle going forward. Here are some action items to be ready for:

- Start thinking about the people you'll want on your core project team.
- Complete the necessary project prep that your agency assigns or that you have to complete internally.
- Begin planning out your weeks to accommodate meetings, internal review time, feedback gathering, etc.
- On this last note, make sure you understand the difference between good and bad feedback. This will make life easier for your agency and will drastically enhance the project.

CHAPTER 5 TAKEAWAYS

The most important takeaways from Chapter 5 involve building your project team. The steps involve the following:

- Narrow down your selection to an ideal team size of no more than five members (three or four if possible). Many successful teams follow the DACI decision-making model, which includes these positions:
  - Driver
  - (Approver) Decider
  - Contributors
  - Informed members
- Identify a strong driver and an empowered decider. (You don't have to be in either of these positions, but there's a good chance you'll be in one of them.)
- Choose additional core project team members wisely.

- Take time to outline additional informed and contributing stakeholders.
- Factor additional stakeholders into an internal communications plan.

As you build your internal project team, be mindful of the following:

- Build accountability structures into your selections and your planning.
- Take the time to build an internal communications plan for any stakeholders that aren't a member of the core project team.

Do not overlook the importance of building your project team. Doing your due diligence here will make a tremendous impact on how your team operates throughout the process.

PART 3

CHAPTER 6

STRATEGY

In Chapter 1, I defined brand as being the perception associated with an organization and everything that represents that. Now it's time to focus on the steps involved in creating a brand, starting with strategy.

To borrow a definition from renowned strategist Marty Neumeier, brand strategy is "a plan for the systematic development of a brand in order to meet business objectives."[8] Within the context of brand building, strategy clarifies the core components of your identity, sheds light on your goals, and provides the core direction to follow while developing a brand's identity. To add some of Focus Lab's spin on this step, the strategy phase is about capturing the essence of your organization, discovering where your company and brand need to be positioned, and outlining a plan for an identity that represents who you are, what you do, and how you wish to be perceived.

---

8   Marty Neumeier, *The Brand Gap: How to Bridge the Distance between Business Strategy and Design*, rev. ed. (Berkeley, CA: New Riders, 2006), 163.

APPROACHING STRATEGY

The ultimate output in this phase is your written strategy. The work itself fulfills a number of important functions and can be a very eye-opening experience for clients: an intensive deep dive into topics that go beyond what many people typically associate with branding.

The strategy phase can feel overwhelming, challenging, and even disruptive at times. After all, it's where your agency learns as much about your company as possible. You may have to answer questions that your company tends to ignore.

STRATEGY IS NOT MARKET RESEARCH

My agency gets the following question every now and again: "Do you do market research?" While we conduct a ton of research, there is a big difference between the research we do and the classical definition of market research. The reason we don't do market research boils down to the differences between branding and marketing.

Remember from earlier, branding draws people to you—and ultimately keeps them coming back. Marketing is a set of activities that tells people about the brand after the fact or based on a campaign. Again, branding is the pull; marketing is the push.

The nature of brand research focuses on what we need to know about YOU in relation to your various business landscapes so we can elevate the version of you that is most true to those areas. Conversely, market research is the research that typically involves things like focus groups, surveys, testing, user interviews, etc. Market research is by design and definition a marketing endeavor. It asks how customers behave in a given situation or how to communicate best with them in another. It is a reactive study of user response, not the proactive gestation of an identity. It does not look into the heart of a brand to ask what its greatest aim in the world is; it only asks if a person likes one thing or another.

The research we do at Focus Lab is direct and covers topics I'll list throughout this chapter. It's qualitative and involves looking at the material you provide, as well as our direct research into your industry, audience groups, and landscapes. This is how we begin to understand those spaces.

DISCOVERY

When faced with a creative problem, the path toward the solution isn't always straight. Strategy helps make sense of the tangle of intersecting issues a brand faces and is in essence the first step of the creative problem solving process first codified in the 1950s by Alex F. Osborn of the internationally renowned advertising agency, BBDO. This process says that in order to solve a creative problem, you must first clarify the issue, understand it specifically, and be sure that it is the correct problem to solve.

Similarly, our philosophy at Focus Lab is that in order to create a solution, we first have to figure out what problems we're solving. That's discovery: uncovering all there is to know about a problem before devising a solution. In order to figure the problems out, we ask a lot of questions, which invariably leads to uncovering even more questions. It's how we gather the deepest insights possible into and about your company and find the questions you and we must answer in order to create a brand that's true to you.

Uncovering the questions behind questions is where the real value of discovery lies. If we were to solve the first problem you present, we would most likely create an incomplete solution. By uncovering all the questions that need answers, we gain a better grasp of the work involved in solving the root problem. How can any agency comprehend the issues you face without also at least glimpsing the questions that you've yet to answer?

If your agency asks you for information even before your project kicks off, there is a reason, and it is in your best interests to answer questions as best as you can. We've had clients ask us, "Why am I doing all this legwork? Isn't this what I hired you for?" This mindset takes me back to something I wrote earlier in the book: never expect your agency to understand your market better than you do.

While efforts and knowledge sharing during discovery can be time consuming, they give your agency key pieces of knowledge, highlight gaps that lead to more questions, and help your agency correctly explore the brand challenges you face.

Strategists take the issue of understanding your brand problem head on. This might seem obvious, but you'd be surprised (or maybe you wouldn't) at how frequently some agencies jump to looking for solutions before they've spent the time it takes to actually understand the real problem. Make sure your agency, even if they don't speak about strategy as we do, understands that just because a company engages with them for a rebrand, it doesn't mean that all they need is new brand assets. It is reasonable to ask your agency how they came to their conclusions, just as it is reasonable for them to ask you to explain all of the factors that should inform your new brand.

GETTING TO THE BRAND PROBLEM

You've chosen to rebrand at this time because on some level, you're aware of having a "brand problem." Regardless of what the issue is, this is an inflection point. If you're working with Focus Lab, then when we first meet with you, we also have an idea as to the nature of your problem. However, we don't begin designing solutions right away.

There is a distinct problem–solution framework at play. No matter who your agency is, when they begin the strategy process, they should explore and frame the big question: what is the brand problem you are facing at this moment? The answer to this question might be simple. More often than not, the issue is deeper below the surface.

It takes the entire strategy process to grasp the problem completely. Have patience as strategy unfolds because getting to the core problem will be the outcome of the work. Once you and your strategists understand the problem at hand, you can take the next steps: articulating your goals, then devising a brand plan to reach them.

To be clear, strategy doesn't have to involve a revelation or even illuminate something new. Sometimes, strategy's job is to confirm your own suspicions about your brand or brand problem. It's not magic. Even when the problem is straightforward, strategy affirms and crystallizes it and makes sure we don't leave out any important considerations.

Before you ruminate on your brand problem, your strategist should help you navigate this. You don't have to have the answers ahead of time. Look forward to strategy as a time of open sharing—a time when you can talk us through the brand conundrums you face and let us do the work of understanding and addressing them.

STRATEGY CLARIFIES CORE COMPONENTS OF IDENTITY

Some clients tell our agency that brand strategy feels like therapy. This might sound cheesy, but it's true. At Focus Lab, this may have to do with our focus on delivering an exceptional client experience, but it's also related to the fact that for many clients, it is the first and maybe only time they've discussed their brand issues with such dedicated focus and with a third party.

A well-done strategy clarifies the core components of your brand's identity. The results point the way forward toward what makes you YOU. Describing an identity is no small feat. You might struggle to put into words precisely how you would communicate the essence of YOU. Just imagine how complex a challenge it can be to capture a company's identity. Yet this is the goal of strategists. They face the challenges of understanding where you've come from, where you're going, what you bring to the table, and how to use this information to get you where you want to go. Their ultimate job is to articulate these pieces in an actionable strategy, which eventually brings the truest version of a brand (an identity) to the world.

In order to do that, strategists, and ultimately writers, must understand and communicate very clearly the core pieces of a brand's identity. For an individual, identity is made up of things like genetics, family dynamics, values, interests, passion, etc. For a brand, identity is similar, composed of values (how we act), passions (purpose), genetics (product, services, core competencies), interests (goals), and even family dynamics (how we relate to the world, differentiation). In this way, the role of strategy is to uncover these pieces of identity and give them visibility.

It can feel amazing to finally have someone with whom you can talk about these things. Together, hearing the challenges people face in their roles and doing it as a unified team in the context of the brand can be a galvanizing, gratifying experience. Strategy makes this experience possible.

THE STRATEGY PROCESS: RESEARCH, EVALUATION, AND DIRECTION

Agencies tackle strategy with various methodologies. At Focus Lab, strategy has three parts: research, evaluation, and direction. These steps combine to lead you into a defined strategic direction, position, and concept for the brand.

RESEARCH

Research is the deep dive into your business: what and who you are, who you are targeting, your industry landscape, and your goals for the future. The overarching goal during this period will be to gain information and insights into all the things that will inform your brand and to uncover any of those pesky unanswered questions. The outcome of this phase is documentation;

its purpose is to reflect back to you everything we learn about you so that we can confirm that we've understood you correctly and are on solid footing for the work to come. Here's what you can expect for yourself and your team during the process:

- You'll be asked a lot of questions and will find yourself thinking pretty deeply about the answers.
- You will be challenged.
- You might land on some big revelations during this time (though these may not be the answers to your big brand questions just yet).

Here's what to expect from your agency:

- They will spend a lot of time listening to you and your team talk about your brand.
- They will bring to light inconsistencies and/or tension between points of research.
- They will read as much internal and external content as they can get their hands on.
- They will dig deeply into the people and companies that directly influence the nature and state of your company's brand—namely, your audiences and your competitors.

And here are some specific topics you can expect to talk about during the research phase:

- Your trajectory (where you've come from and where you're going)
- Your existing brand identity
- Your audiences, their pain points, demographics, and psychographics

- Your direct and indirect competition
- Attributes that describe how you wish to be perceived
- Core messages like purpose, mission, and vision
- Your present and future positioning
- Your brand architecture
- Misconceptions about you and things to avoid
- Where your existing brand falls short of the needs you have now and your needs for the future

At Focus Lab, when we ask these questions and discuss these topics with you, we are also building that documentation we mentioned above: the research and evaluation document. From there, we'll take a look at what we've learned about who you are now with where you want to go and identify where your brand opportunities lie.

There is a number of reasons why we spend so much time researching and documenting during the strategy phase. For starters, this is how we confirm with you everything we've learned. It also helps ensure that we look at everything through our brand strategy lens. That way, we see where your brand isn't serving you or taking you where you want to go.

EVALUATION

Evaluation is a careful consideration of the research in light of your goals. It explores opportunities for the future and provides the first inklings of what the strategist will recommend as part of direction.

Research (along with its documentation) and evaluation go hand in hand: R&E. Focus Lab's process intertwines the two at roughly the same time. Research reflects back what we've heard from you, while evaluation looks at that research and asks what might need to change in order to meet your brand goals. Therefore, we evaluate and document what's working and what's not working in areas such as the following:

- Your existing visual and verbal identity
- Your competitors' visual and verbal identities
- How well you're appealing to your audience's needs
- Your apparent positioning amidst the competition
- Your differentiation
- Your brand architecture

We also consider new opportunities that might come to light during the process—ideas that were not captured earlier in your stated brand goals. Whenever we see opportunities, or pitfalls for that matter, we document it for you in R&E. On that note, R&E is heavy on the research and documentation, and it remains an open process. In other words, these insights will be available to you along the way. You'll also come to certain realizations on your own simply by having the research presented back to you.

We've seen plenty of cases where people inside of companies perceive their brand much differently from one another. An added benefit of this phase is that research and evaluation highlight contradictions or misalignments. It can be enlightening to see multiple, preexisting perceptions of your brand reflected back to you.

DIRECTION

By this point, you will have read the research and seen the evaluation. All of that work results in the final step of this phase: the proposed direction. This is the culminating piece of strategy recommendation for your brand—the direction that you will see come to life throughout the subsequent brand deliverables.

Direction summarizes who you are and where you are going and makes clear recommendations for how to get there. As a written summary document, it is the foundation for the transition to visual and verbal brand outcomes. In short, direction is your new north star, your beacon for the brand path ahead, and your litmus test for all your brand outcomes. Specifically, direction clarifies the following:

- The solution to your brand problem(s)
- The path to achieving your brand goals
- Your target audience
- Your brand's opportunity in its competitive space
- Your brand positioning and differentiation

Direction also includes strategic and practical recommendations for how the new brand will deliver on your goals, appeal to your best-fit audiences, stand out from competitors, and showcase your ownable differentiation. At Focus Lab, before we create anything on behalf of your brand, we "ask" direction if the work lines up:

- Do our logo explorations align with our strategic findings?
- What does direction say about the emotion we wish to evoke?
- Does this piece of messaging reflect our position accurately?

- Will these colorways appeal to our audience in the right ways?
- Are our attributes evident in this new identity?

Adhering to direction continues well after you launch your rebrand. Years later, when it's time to extend your brand, you will share the direction document with your team to ensure that what they create aligns with its directives. In other words, every new idea should come from the same core foundation, and nothing should be *so new* that it comes from nowhere.

THE WRAP ON STRATEGY

Without a thoughtful strategy, your rebrand is just creativity for creativity's sake—devoid of meaning and lacking connection to your company's ethos. The new brand may initially come together faster if you skip strategy, but it will miss out and lack the impact your organization is hungry for.

Strategy brings rationale to the table. It forms the basis for decision-making as things begin to play out in real time. All of the research, discussions, team-building exercises and internal communication help create the ONE PIECE against which all your future brand work will be measured. Use this knowledge of how we do strategy at Focus Lab to inform your thinking as you approach your own brand project. If you're not working with us, be sure you ask your agency for a strategic guidepost— something against which to measure the relevance and success of the brand outcomes.

As I finish strategy, I want to call out the fact that this book is reaching its own inflection point—the narrative is about to move from the theoretical (strategy) to the practical (communications and design). In order to make the most of the strategy conversation, let's remember how Marty Neumeier puts it in *The Brand Gap*:

> Unfortunately, the left brain doesn't always know what the right brain is doing. Whenever there's a rift between strategy and creativity—between logic and magic—there's a brand gap. It can cause a brilliant strategy to fail where it counts most, at the point of contact with the customer, or it can doom a bold creative initiative before it's even launched, way back at the planning stage.[9]

In short, there's no point in doing all of this wonderful discovery and strategy work unless you plan to capitalize on it.

---

9   Neumeier, *The Brand Gap*, 15.

CHAPTER 7

COMMUNICATIONS (YOUR VERBAL IDENTITY)

Often overlooked in relation to the design elements of a rebrand, communications (or comms) actually carries as much weight, if not more.[10] If you agree with this statement, here's a standing ovation for you. If this is a surprise, then congratulations because you are learning a core brand truth: the verbal and written aspects of a brand—those words that take every piece of identity and articulate them—are integral to your brand success.

Let me set one expectation right away. Clients often read "communications" and assume that this work results in messages (taglines, billboard copy, or other marketing outputs). In the strict context of brand and branding, the work of comms does not equal *messages* but *messaging*: the identity and concepts

---

10 Judith Kraus et al., "Bringing Research Alive through Stories: Reflecting on Research Storytelling as a Public Engagement Method," *Research for All* 6, no. 1 (2022), https://doi.org/10.14324/RFA.06.1.20.

behind the marketing messages you will eventually share out in the word.

In this chapter, my focus is on the core (internal) written and verbal elements of your brand on which external messages are based. At Focus Lab, we call this "brand writing," and you will see this phrase throughout the chapter.

APPROACHING BRAND WRITING

In Chapter 6, I wrote that strategy illuminates various components of identity. At Focus Lab, a writer is always part of the strategy process as our team builds out core pieces of your identity. The moment that our writers begin writing things down, the work is already transitioning from being a conceptual definition of identity (intangibles) to a written one. This is the beginning of the verbal part of your identity. Once we enter the comms phase, we continue to flesh out your verbal brand assets. In that way, brand writing is a derivative of strategy. Ultimately, brand writing sets you and anyone communicating on your behalf up for success whenever they begin crafting written messages and content.

WRITING IS A PARTNER TO STRATEGY

As strategy wraps up and direction becomes clear, brand writing helps to resolve two key points before the strategy work is complete:

- How are you differentiated?
- How are you positioned?

It also seeks to articulate four key aspects of your identity:

- Who are you, what do you do, and why? (Core messages, ethos)
- What principles guide your actions? (Values)
- How do you relate to your landscape? (Relationship and situational dynamics)
- How are you personified? (Voice and tone)

MESSAGING VS. MESSAGES

Things can get tricky during this phase because it's tempting to take written words and turn them into messages, especially if you fall in love with something right away. It's important to draw the distinction between the words that define your brand identity (messaging) and the words that communicate your identity to the world (messages).

This might seem like I'm splitting hairs, but trust me. Our agency has seen plenty of situations where clients expect to walk away from a brand project with pockets full of messages. What they don't realize is that an exercise in brand is an exercise in identity, not in marketing. Communicating that identity via messages happens later.

Our goal during brand writing is to nail the underlying messaging that articulates the truest version of your company. This work is more about function than form. Will the messaging work show up on a billboard? Can it transition into web copy? These questions don't concern us during the brand writing phase, and they shouldn't concern you either because the work is about bringing the real you to the surface, then to the world. Here are some examples to illustrate this difference:

From Kion, a Cloud Enablement Provider and Former Focus Lab Client

Messaging:

- *Vision: To transform organizations by empowering their people to move farther and faster in the cloud.*
- *Mission: Make it simpler and easier for organizations to achieve the benefits of the cloud.*

Site headlines (messages) that derive from that messaging:

- "We're on a mission to make the cloud easier for everyone."
- "Unlock the promise of the cloud, all in one place."

From Focus Lab's Brand Work

Messaging:

- *Mission: Our mission is to use our expertise and passion for branding to unlock the potential of organizations and people around us.*

Site copy (messages) that derive from that messaging:

- "If these brand opportunities could unlock potential in your business, reach out and tell us your story."

Still, you might actually fall in love with some messaging and want to use certain passages verbatim in a press release or on a splash page. That's great, but our concern is to make sure your messaging is right. Your project scope might include actual messages like taglines and public-facing values definitions. This is also okay, but again, these are outcomes of solid messaging, but in and of themselves they are not central to your identity.

THE BRAND WRITING PROCESS

If you work with Focus Lab, the person who's in charge of your communications work is your brand writer. Our writers possess deep academic knowledge of writing and a breadth of experience in brand. They take direction from strategists and continue to build branded verbal identity assets accordingly. At the end of the brand writing phase at our agency, you will have received the following:

- Written clarity of what you do and what you offer to the world.
- Unity around one set of foundational statements.
- Written value of your offering in direct and compelling terms.
- Guidelines for engaging your audience by speaking to their shared concerns, pain points, and needs.
- Concepts or themes critical to your differentiation and positioning.
- Clarity on any aspects of your identity that are misunderstood or overlooked (breadth of expertise, scope of offering, etc.).

POSITIONING AND DIFFERENTIATION

In brand, positioning outlines the place your company occupies in the minds, hearts, and lives of your audience. Positioning your company for the future is essential before any successful brand work can be complete. Positioning straddles the line between strategy (the future) and writing (articulating that position), and we consider it a shared exercise between strategist and writer that aims to achieve one of two goals:

1. To find and label a point of differentiation that already exists within your business and brand; or
2. To define a new point of differentiation on which to base your brand and its strategy.

Either way, the purpose of positioning is to examine your differentiation, illuminate what makes you stand out in the eyes of customers, and develop key pieces that accentuate your brand position in such a way that it creates a compelling difference. Our agency puts a lot of weight on differentiation. Identifying what's unique forces us to look beyond the objective, which is where the greatest potential exists for cementing your perception in the minds of your audience. This work clarifies a number of things, including:

- Your target market and segment (and their needs)
- Your competitive category and differentiation
- The proof of your promise

Different agencies approach positioning in different ways. But regardless of the method, be sure that you and they resolve positioning your brand for the future before the remainder of the brand is created. One quick point here: Positioning in the context of a brand is sometimes, but not always, the same as positioning in the greater context of a business. Whereas business, product, or service positioning defines how you conceive of your offerings in response to a market, brand positioning looks at that strategy but is focused on what we need to differentiate your brand in relation to your competition.

CORE MESSAGING

Since brand is identity. During brand writing, we need to take various aspects of identity and articulate them with words. For most organizations, these four core messages serve as a brand's backbone:

- Purpose
- Mission
- Vision
- Values

They explain why you exist, what you do, the impact you hope to make on the world, and the principles that guide you. To borrow from Simon Sinek again, these are your Golden Circle: your Why, your What, and your How.

No matter which model you prefer, the intent is the same: to capture your essence and explain what you bring to the world in a few succinct statements. Ultimately, when taken together with your basic visual identity elements (Chapter 8), they communicate to the world who you are and what you are about. They also tell your target audience why they should care and what's in it for them.

With Focus Lab, expect to spend some time looking specifically at purpose, mission, vision, and values. Even if you already have these statements, it's important that we review them critically in light of your new brand strategy to ensure they are still true to you now and align with your strategic map for the future.

SITUATIONAL MESSAGING

We use the term "situational messaging" to describe two statements that help a brand relate to the spaces in which it operates: value proposition and unique selling proposition. These derive from the four core messages above and add an additional layer of taking the audience into account.

In Focus Lab's view, producing these statements is the first step in relating what you bring to your audience in a way that is meaningful to them. They become part of your verbal brand assets and can help you create messages that resonate in different marketing channels. Again, it's fine if you decide to put aspects of situational messaging on your website, for instance, but we don't write them with this in mind.

AUDIENCE MESSAGING

Audience messaging is another extension of your brand identity related to specific audience groups. Think of it as a matrix of different questions and answers, created in a way that gives you a reference document for communicating with each audience. Agencies approach audience messaging in a number of ways, and audience messaging exercises vary quite a bit. Our agency's exercise asks the following:

- Who are your primary audience groups?
- What are their needs and pain points?
- What do we offer that satisfies their needs or alleviates their pain points?
- What benefit do they receive as a result of having those needs met?
- How can we best communicate those benefits to them?

The outcome and purpose of this work is to provide guidelines for communicating with your primary audience groups with the messages, themes, phrasing, and emphasis that speak to them in ways they find meaningful.

BRAND VOICE

As brand terms go, "voice" gets tossed around a lot and is often misused. Focus Lab defines voice as the personality and character that are evident in your communication. We often use famous personalities to help hone in on the right voice for your brand. If your brand were personified, what or who would it sound like? To help explain, let's consider two famous personalities that have distinct styles of communication:

- Anthony Bourdain had the ability to explain heavy concepts in a way that was accessible and also edgy.
- Neil deGrasse Tyson can convey subject matter authority but in a way that is thoughtful and contextual.

Assuming you're a B2B brand, does it make sense for your brand to sound like Bugs Bunny? Probably not. Your core messages could be completely accurate representations of you and your ethos, but if you present them in a voice that doesn't represent the character of your brand, your message will suffer because the characterization isn't right. On that note, the work of defining your voice should consider what will resonate with your audience as well.

Our agency also considers your brand archetype when defining voice. Without going into too many details, archetypes are universal character models and iconic narratives that represent prevailing experiences throughout human history (like "the hero," "everyman," "the rebel," etc.). Archetypes are useful in branding because they provide additional details to lean into as you build out characteristics, behaviors, etc. and because they provide models that people relate to.

We can use details of your brand's archetype to inform descriptors or voice, helping us stay true to the qualities that characterize your organization. Some archetypes you might not know you know include:

- Disney, which embodies the magician archetype, creates memorable moments through dreamlike experiences.
- Old Spice's jester archetype is full of pranks and mischief and never takes itself too seriously.
- IBM's sage archetype creates solutions driven by research and mastery.

In the end, voice is essential because people buy from brands they know, like, and trust. And how does this happen?

- They get to know a brand through consistent, ownable verbal representation, along with opportunities for interaction.

- They begin to like or even love a brand when it talks in a tone they relate to about things they care about.
- They trust a brand when it is consistent in how it upholds its values, covers topics of interest, and sounds "like itself" no matter where people interact with it.

Like other elements of your brand, accurate representation ensures that you are presenting the truest version of you, while consistent usage and application inspire trust and confidence and build brand equity.

BRAND NARRATIVE AND STORY

People crave stories—it's human nature. Whether you're listening to a storyteller, watching a movie, or reading a book, chances are you can't help but to look for pieces of the story with which you identify or relate. Much like archetypes tell us about common human models, narratives lead us to concepts— mental models that represent relatable problems. And it's not just our nature; there's even science that shows the value of stories in creating engagement and recall of content.[11]

Without a clear, compelling story, a brand leaves it up to customers to fill the gaps. To truly move people and to move your brand into action, you need to tell your story in a compelling way. During the strategy phase, your strategist helps to find the roots of your story by framing your inflection point through a brand lens. In the brand writing (communications) phase, your brand writer picks up the story torch and goes forward, drafting a narrative or concept that characterizes your brand's inflection point.

---

11   Kraus et al., "Bringing Research Alive through Stories."

- The writer documents this narrative in a way that helps explain the visual work you will see during the design phase (Chapter 8), e.g. *"With a nod to the familiar signs, shapes, and symbols that guide us through our everyday lives, this expression positions Locally as the world's de facto online-to-offline shopping network."*
- The writer and designer continue to use this narrative, or multiple manifestations of the same narrative, as inspiration for all design and communications work to come.
- Your writer continues to refine and document this narrative throughout the design phase. This material ultimately becomes your brand story.

People define "brand story" in many ways. What does this mean for your business if you have one primary narrative or concept? In essence, your brand story is your brand narrative; however, the way in which your agency writes a final, formal "brand story" document can vary based on how you intend to use it.

Some companies want to publish their brand story on their website for all to see. Others like the idea of drafting the story for internal use only, to help build brand ambassadors before sharing their new identity with the world. The basic narrative is the same, but the way in which it is told can vary depending on the intended audience and usage.

STYLE

As a part of the brand writing work, Focus Lab's writers also catalog stylistic choices that help guide and define how you communicate in writing. These include things like punctuation preferences (like the Oxford comma), word lists (terms to use/avoid), inclusivity (using gender neutral words), and so on. Ultimately this results in a style manual. Generally, the content of this manual doesn't require revision, but Focus Lab produces one to catch and document stylistic rules that add definition and color to your written communication.

CONCEPTS AND EXPRESSIONS

This topic bridges strategy, writing, and design. I'm including it here because at Focus Lab the writer is the one who produces most of this work, even though it's a shared effort. On the written, conceptual side, the team identifies concepts that help communicate the essence of your brand and then propose expressions that might help illustrate it. On the visual side, the team decides which expressions communicate that essence best and use those as a foundation for visual design exploration. (More on this in Chapter 8.)

"Concepting" is an exercise that helps transition from ideas (strategy and writing) to visuals (design). Agencies have to be able to make a strategic argument for any visual recommendations, and concepting helps do that. Discussing abstractions like concepts can get complicated. To simplify, we work to identify concepts that help tell a client's story in a way that their audience will find compelling.

Abstract concepts and expressions can help us tell a story because they give us a new lens through which to consider a situation or a theme. One example of an abstract concept is "community."

On its own, "community" is abstract, even if its interpretations are quite literal. You could extrapolate "community" into many expressions: a gathering house, a sanctuary, a map of localities, an image of people holding hands. There are endless visual ways to express "community." Which one is most accurate depends on the situation.

This work helps us make the transition from the theoretical to the visual. Also, agencies use the term "concept" differently. If the term comes up, find out how your agency defines it.

HOW TO REVIEW BRAND WRITING WORK

Being the first non-strategy work you will see, writing deliverables are the earliest actual brand outcomes. The rubber is clearly meeting the road at this point, and you'll gain a true understanding of your depth of collaboration and mental investment.

It's your agency's job to turn big, abstract ideas into messaging that aligns with the heart of your company. It's your job to help them do it. It will take a few iterations before you and your agency nail down this phase. You and your team are going to be just as involved during brand writing as you are in every other phase, even if you don't have someone on your core project team whose role aligns with brand writing.

Most people enter a rebrand with visuals in mind. If you're itching to get past brand writing so you can finally see designs, you are not alone. Design tends to feel more accessible and universal, and many people have visceral reactions to it. On the other hand, writing requires an understanding of grammar, vocabulary around semantics, and other details that can make it harder to engage with.

When words are the focus, you can almost always count on there being some moments of splitting hairs. Reviewing words requires your team to align on your core components of identity (which are complex) as well as the way you wish to communicate these components. Even though people prefer to hold "communications" at arm's length when faced with the full comms deliverable, people can become backseat drivers. Suddenly, everyone is a writer. People dust off their old college notebooks, reach for their trusty thesaurus, and start editing. This is another one of those "human nature" situations.

The thing is, your agency does not need you to engage at this level. At Focus Lab, we don't expect you or anyone on your team to be an expert grammarian or to do any writing for us. With each week's deliverable, we understand that some clients want to review the content in as detailed a manner as possible. However, it's not your responsibility to be a wordsmith or to edit the content. That job belongs to the brand writer. Your main responsibility is to let our writers know two things:

1. When the meaning of something they've written is inaccurate or doesn't align with the truth of your brand.
2. How and why it's inaccurate or doesn't align.

Providing these insights might sound easy, but this work can actually be difficult to articulate. In fact, what many clients struggle with is the fact that it's easy to point out the things they don't like, but it's much harder to articulate *why* something isn't right. If you find yourself in this situation, refer back to Chapter 4's section about providing good feedback. Here are some pointers specific to brand writing:

- When you review brand writing work, base your feedback on how successful the work is compared to its goals.
- Include a thoughtful explanation of why something is or isn't successful.
- Let the writer do the wordsmithing and editing necessary to satisfy your feedback.
- Keep in mind that the brand writers are experts in writing. They will guide you through the pieces of the work that need to be wordsmithed and those that don't. Trust your writers for their expertise.
- Remember that the writing pieces you receive are not yet messages (which I detailed at the start of this chapter). They aren't meant to go on billboards or T-shirts (unless you *really* want to use them). During the brand writing phase, they are capturing the essence of your brand.
- In the end, accuracy is more important than poetry during brand writing.

Keep in mind that struggling during the first few rounds of review is a normal and even healthy part of the process. The main point I want to bring to the conversation is how review and iteration during brand writing tends to be different than how review and iteration go during the design phase. Finally, here are some specific questions to ask when reviewing actual communications deliverables:

- Do these words describe your brand in a way that you and others have not been able to do in the past?
- Do they successfully represent your brand attributes and/ or archetype?
- Can you imagine the ways in which this messaging will begin to translate into broader marketing messages?

- Does the messaging sound like a better, more aspirational version of you?

It's okay if you don't love every word you see the first time you see it. Focus Lab's process is heavy on iteration. We know that sometimes we need to put certain words on paper to get feedback before we can hone in on the very best statement. The goal is to start each step of the process, then build toward a final solution via input and feedback.

THE WRAP ON BRAND WRITING

The relationship between strategy and brand writing can't be overstated. Moving from writing to visual design—I'll continue this line of thinking—to help you gain a better sense of how your verbal and written messages run in parallel with the visual components. In fact, it's safe to say that you'll most likely review verbal and visual design pieces in tandem. One important difference to keep in mind, though, is that while brand communications work at Focus Lab is largely focused on that messaging (the statements that may become public facing but aren't written to be), visual design *is* focused on visible outputs. This is an important distinction that will help you manage your expectations for each set of work.

When the verbal and visual identity pieces stay rooted in the process that started with discovery and moved through strategy, your brand continues to build upon itself nicely. On that note, let's move into the visual design phase, where the same concepts your agency unpacks as part of brand writing find their way into visual form.

CHAPTER 8

DESIGN (YOUR VISUAL IDENTITY)

Everything you've done since onboarding has built to this next phase of the project—the visual expression of your brand. Sometimes referred to simply as "design," the visual components of your brand continue to carry and build on the brand narrative (Chapter 7).

As I shared in the introduction, many people give visual design the most attention and emphasis during a brand project. It's the most common brand element we interface with, and it feels easy to critique. However, a brand cannot be boiled down to just a logo or any other design element. Visual design can only truly be understood and appreciated when considered in light of all the earlier steps.

A number of elements make up the foundation of your visual identity. They create your visual identity system. Each adds another layer of expression that supports the larger narrative taking shape in your rebrand. Your agency will address these and more during design, including:

- Logo, including a mark and/or logotype
- Primary and supporting color palettes
- Typography system
- Photography, illustration, and patterns
- Iconography style
- Broader visual language elements

These components build upon the communications work to establish a throughline of verbal and visual storytelling.

Close your eyes and imagine you've just walked into a Starbucks. What visual elements do you see? Is it their prominent green? The iconic mermaid logo? Maybe it's the varied woods they use throughout their stores to create a sense of comfort? Each of these visual decisions has a basis in strategy and plays an important role in the visual system.

APPROACHING VISUAL DESIGN

The progression from strategy, to writing, to design is cumulative. They happen in this order because it's a way to learn, develop, and cement concepts and directions in a responsive, targeted way. Just as writing builds on strategy, design builds on writing by taking the written elements forward into visual manifestations. When your words come first, visual design flows in an intentional and logical way. That way, by the time design starts, we have already been working with your core messaging (mission, purpose, vision). Remember we call these "core" pieces because they are central to identity.

Could an agency create a visual representation of identity without first understanding what your brand is all about? Not successfully, or in a way that captures everything your organization represents. When an agency starts with design before comms (or worse, before strategy) they wind up trying to retrofit various brand attributes around the visuals. The results are noticeably confusing and forced, often a result of the design being driven by bias or personal taste rather than strategic intention.

THE IMPORTANCE OF LOGO MARKS

Stop me if you've heard or even said the following: "Our company is changing; we need a new logo!" I hear it often. Everyone wants an iconic logo—their own special Nike swoosh. Unfortunately, this misses the bigger picture and the true impact of a successful rebrand.

Your logo matters, but not in the way you may think. In the words of brand icon Michael Bierut, "It [brand-new logo] is an empty vessel awaiting the meaning that will be poured into it by history and experience."[12] On its own, your logo has no meaning, especially when it's shiny and new. In fact, your logo isn't meant to have its own unique meaning.

Will your updated or brand-new logo be beautiful and ultimately serve as a symbol of your rebrand? Yes. Will it be packed with emotion and valuable memories for your customers to draw upon? No, at least not at the start.

---

12   Michael Bierut, *How to Use Graphic Design to Sell Things, Explain Things, Make Things Look Better, Make People Laugh, Make People Cry, and (Every Once in a While) Change the World* (New York: Harper Design, 2015), 179.

YOUR LOGO IS NOT YOUR FOUNDATION. YOUR BRAND IS.

Great brands are not built on the backs of logos. It's the opposite; logos are built to help symbolize great brands. We all experience brands throughout our lives. As various experiences take shape, our perceptions become baked into logos, for better or worse. If an alien arrived on earth and saw the Rolex or Apple logos, it would have no idea what the company does.

The longer we live with a brand, the more its logo evolves into a deeper story and becomes a symbol with its own personal meaning. The most powerful logos in the world pull meaning from the brand they've represented over long periods of time. They are the vessel of that brand, successfully carrying its meaning in a recognizable shape.

Let me come back to Nike again. The swoosh has been around since 1971. When designer Carolyn Davidson created it, she was trying to embody a sense of motion and speed. Is "motion" the first thing you think of when you see the swoosh today? By now, Nike's logo carries many other emotional connections, and the original idea that drove the logo's design has given way to what the brand has become.

This idea illustrates my key point: Your logo is not your brand's most important asset. It cannot represent all that you are. Its purpose is simpler—to be a beacon and identifier. It is not the determinant of your future success.

Focus Lab has had plenty of projects where executives get unsettled because they want the logo to represent every line in the story they were telling. We help clients navigate this fear with examples like Nike and Chase Bank and can say confidently that this kind of thinking is a fool's errand. You can't possibly plan for or imagine all the meanings people will create and associate with your brand once they experience it in full.

Whenever we've had to hope that a logo will eventually win over a founder post-launch, it has. Seeing a brand come to life and discovering what it provides a company will do that. The magic is that by letting a logo do its job (identification within the brand system), one day it will come to represent more.

Here's a different company on the other end of the logo spectrum: Craigslist. Can you picture their logo? They are very successful despite the near-total absence of a logo. I actually had to look it up. It's a purple peace sign that they don't even use on their website. (It only shows up as a favicon in the left of the browser tab.) This example reinforces my point: Your logo will not determine the success of your business. You can have a great logo and be unsuccessful just as easily as you can have no logo and reach upwards of 80 percent profit on an estimated $1 billion in revenue like Craigslist.[13]

In the end, your logo's design should get special attention, and your agency should account for recognition, scalability and a number of other design technicalities. Still, don't get stuck thinking or demanding that your agency's designers build a logo or any other single piece of a brand system that expresses *every* brand attribute, explains what your business does at first

---

13   Sara Salinas. "Craigslist Is Raking in $1 Billion a Year, According to One Researcher's Estimates," *CNBC*, January 24, 2019, https://www.cnbc.com/2019/01/24/craigslist-posts-annual-revenue-of-1-billion-study.html; AIM Group, "Craigslist Revenue Rebounds; Traffic Slide Continues," PR Newswire, news release, February 08, 2022. https://www.prnewswire.com/news-releases/craigslist-revenue-rebounds-traffic-slide-continues-301477660.html#:~:text=The%20AIM%20Group%20has%20estimated,at%2070%25%20to%2080%25.

glance, simultaneously speaks to every audience, and stands out as being simple and iconic. Let your agency build a vessel, and allow the vessel to fill with meaning over time.

DIFFERENTIATION IN VISUAL DESIGN

I talked about differentiation in Chapter 7 and want to bring it up again as part of the visual design conversation. In his book *The Purple Cow*, Seth Godin explains that, "In a crowded marketplace, fitting in is failing. In a busy marketplace, not standing out is the same as being invisible."[14] This is true from all angles of your business, including how you are positioned in your market. But what does standing out or differentiating mean within the realm of design? Is it paramount to success, or just a "nice to have" situation?

Being clearly identifiable as "different" through the lens of design will help your brand stand out in a sea of sameness. It's a way to start your customers down the psychological path of wondering why you are different. Here are a few points to consider as you determine how differentiated (or not) the visual aspects of your brand should be.

CONSIDER OPPORTUNITIES

You will have had the chance to review and consider different opportunities during the strategy phase. Perhaps all the other companies in your vertical lean heavily toward blue, and your agency encourages you to consider a different color. Maybe the companies in your competitive landscape have jumped on

---

14   Seth Godin, *The Purple Cow: Transform Your Business by Being Remarkable* (New York: Portfolio, 2003).

a trend of using a modern sans serif typeface, and choosing a serif could differentiate your brand while nodding to the intellect of your offering. As you consider opportunities, remember that your design system components work together to tell the whole story. When the entire industry starts to look the same, you run the risk of feeling like a commodity, rather than having a unique, purposeful offering.

There are many ways to differentiate. What will happen if a certain aspect of your design is the same as your competition? Depending on your current position in the market, having similarities to the competition might actually help you.

ADDRESS "OWNABILITY"

The notion of "ownability" is a common misconception about design assets. Let's use color to highlight this point. At Focus Lab, we'll hear things like, "We want to achieve the recognizability of Tiffany." Our answer is usually something like, "It took more than a century of consistency and marketing for them to get there."

Being able to "own" a color can be a strong asset. Is it possible? Some brands have trademarked various colors, but that doesn't equate to complete ownership. Nickelodeon probably couldn't stop The Home Depot from using orange, for instance. These companies operate in vastly different industries, and their use of similar shades of the same color is unlikely to create customer confusion.

To be clear, choosing brand elements based on what you can own should not be your goal. You should focus on what's realistic and achievable; do your best to capture something unique in your space, and make sure it matches your attributes and brand story. Ownability may come in time, but it doesn't determine success in the long run. Nor is it something you can predict or obtain in the middle of a rebrand.

VARIATION MATTERS

What happens when you find the right color for your brand, only to realize someone in your competitive landscape is already using it? This is where an iterative process like Focus Lab's shines. It's also a reminder that brands are larger than any one single element. Facebook, LinkedIn, and Twitter are good examples. They all use blue, and they're all social media based, yet they're able to grow market share, tell different stories, provide unique selling propositions, and resonate with varied audiences. If blue is indeed right for *all* of them, there is no need for *any* of them to shift to pink just to look different. That would likely have more negative implications than running the risk of looking the same because of color.

As you review color choices, it's worth asking whether or not a certain color supports and elevates your brand story. If it does, and the shade and execution are different from others in your competitive landscape, then you are on the right track. Remember your brand's ultimate uniqueness exists in the entire brand ecosystem, not just color, typography, or any other single element. I assure you that Starbucks isn't the only coffee brand that uses some version of green.

THE VISUAL DESIGN PROCESS

To discuss what it takes to build a successful visual identity that embodies your mission, speaks to your customers, and represents your products, I'd like to lean into Focus Lab's process. We break things down across two high-level phases: visual strategy and visual design.

VISUAL STRATEGY

Since visual design is cumulative, our agency wants to be sure that our findings and directions from one phase carry through to the next. Therefore, we emphasize visual strategy as a way to bridge the written, theoretical work of strategy and comms, and the visual, practical manifestations of design. Not all agencies take this approach. We believe visual strategy is a necessary step that creates a more efficient transition to visual design.

Our methodology takes different forms, depending on the client and the brand problem we're trying to solve. Regardless of the exact methodology we follow, visual strategy always references the deeper brand strategy, including all the concepts, attributes, and archetypes we've uncovered to date.

Moodboards During Visual Strategy

Moodboards are the main deliverables during visual strategy. Each moodboard captures a distinct visual direction we envision for your brand. If you're not familiar with a moodboard, think of a collage that displays a variety of visual elements, including colors, shapes, fonts, patterns, textures, and more.

Different visuals mean different things to people. One person may hear "bold" and think "black and white," while another person hears it and thinks, "vibrant and colorful." The moodboards help us zero in on interpretations, ensure that we're aligned with strategy, and focus our lens before we dive deeper into visual design.

You'll receive multiple moodboards to review during this phase, each consisting of images that represent different strategic directions. Your main task is to tell us which one, or which aspects within each of them, feel like they could lead to an accurate visual representation of your brand.

VISUAL DESIGN

Once we receive your notes, meet with you to discuss the visual strategy, and get clear direction for next steps, we begin the actual visual design. Sometimes, the visual design process will be linear, but let me be clear that visual design is hardly a one-size-fits-all operation. The easiest way to illustrate this point is using the examples of a logomark (shape or icon) or a logotype (the words or letters of the brand's name).

Typically, we'll have strategic direction for a logomark or logotype by the time we wrap up visual strategy. Until we put design tools to use to present them visually, we will not have made any design decisions about these visuals. We don't know for sure which elements your brand will require until we've started the work. Of course, we know that you will end up with a logo, colors, fonts, etc. but the act of producing them and figuring out how they balance in the brand (which one has more weight, which is secondary, etc.) requires flexibility and iteration.

Iteration Remains Key

We use the term "round" to describe, in our cadence, a week's worth of work and the subsequent deliverable. Each round in visual design builds on the previous and drives the iterative process. We work with your feedback and also build on our own ideas for original design work. As we present each round, we work toward isolating, balancing, and finalizing each design element.

The First Round

Having defined your visual mood during the visual strategy phase, round one of visual design shows this mood through various interpretations of your brand concept. Again, our methodology varies from client to client, but the throughline of the concept will be present.

Most often, your project's strategist, writer, and designer will have extrapolated this conceptual idea into multiple visual expressions. Now they are ready to present these expressions in a way that pairs narrative and design. There's no hard-and-fast rule for exactly which visual elements you'll see in the first round, and you'll most likely see a few concepts. You can almost always expect logo and color exploration to show up here and very likely some typography systems as well.

Early Rounds

Let's say you liked some of what you saw during the first round but weren't too excited about all of it. That's okay. As long as you share good, honest feedback, you will start to see things take shape as the weeks progress. With that said, you can expect the first round, as well as the early rounds that follow, to include a lot of exploration as we settle in on your color, type, patterns, hierarchy, photography, illustration, and more.

Later Rounds

While the early rounds focus on exploration, later rounds are all about refinement. This is where we fine-tune the decisions and feedback from the early rounds. Depending on the complexity of your brand architecture or the type of brand system you need, the later rounds are when we begin to look at existing sub-brands as well as additional brand extensions (such as product logos, avatars and icons, patterns, etc.).

Throughout every round, your main task is to provide the type of actionable, consistent feedback I wrote about in Chapter 4. In just a minute I'll also cover feedback specific to design deliverables.

Receiving Final Assets and Guidelines

When design wraps up, you will have seen and approved all visual pieces of your brand, and the designer will transition into the steps that bring those all together in an organized file system and those final usage rules. Eventually, you will receive the finalized brand elements and assets, plus rules and guidelines for applying them, as part of your brand style guide. I'll share specific details about the style guide in Chapter 9.

REVIEWING VISUAL DESIGN DELIVERABLES

The entire brand process includes decisions at every turn.

Back during strategy and comms, you and your team success-fully navigated the tricky terrain of choices and leaned in one direction or the other. Perhaps those choices came easily as you focused on the verbal and written aspects of your identity. What I've discovered and what Focus Lab has encountered many times is that the decision-making process in the visual design phase usually feels different and often skews toward a difficult impasse.

Clients report that reviewing and settling on design feel binary, weighty, risky. This makes sense. After all, during strategy and comms, your strategist and writer use lots of words and con-cepts to represent identity. During design, your creative team uses a handful of very explicit shapes, colors, and moods to visualize big ideas—and asks you to choose!

At this point, you're also on a dual track of reviewing writing and design deliverables. Meanwhile, the launch date is closing in. The visual side of your review work can become nerve-racking, and focusing on fine details can start to feel monotonous. This brings to mind something known as the Ellsberg paradox.

In decision theory, this concept suggests that when choosing between two things, one with a known level of risk, the other with an unknown level of risk, people often choose the known risk (even if the latter has the potential for greater reward). In this example, design decisions can often translate into trend-ing more safe (known) versus new and different (unknown). I bring this up because if we can actually quantify risk, we can lead ourselves toward a more confident decision.

You always knew there were going to be risks in your rebrand—

some big, some small. If you've arrived at the visual design phase, then you have already stared down a number of them. Now is the time to remember all those intelligent steps you've taken and use this memory to put your fears aside. One of the best ways to confront and power through moments of uncertainty is to come back to a core question: is this design successful in meeting its goals? This is much different than asking "Is it good?" or worse, "Do I like it?" When you gauge a deliverable on how well it meets the goals outlined in strategy and the identity clarified during brand writing, you take micro-steps toward reducing risk.

This is not arithmetic, but it is an objective methodology wrapped around solving a subjective problem. By applying it to your design review, you move toward building a brand that's based on reason, rationale, and strategic thinking rather than personal preference and chance.

1. BEWARE OF THE SAFETY TRAP

Similar to the Ellsberg paradox, the certainty effect suggests that we feel more favorably toward decisions that yield certain (predictable, expected, etc.) outcomes, than those with uncertain outcomes. This tendency causes one problem in particular for brands. Think back to what I wrote in Chapter 2 about the ROI of a rebrand. Now that you've read this far, I assume you trust that you can actualize enough of a return. However, the design phase is the moment when many clients begin remembering why they signed on for this project in the first place. All these highly visible decisions (colors, images, typeface, etc.) begin to frighten people into playing it safe. Yet, brave options can bring greater rewards.

Challenge yourself and your agency to imagine and prove the possibilities for what you stand to gain. Force yourself to look for the opportunity to win, rather than holding on tightly to things you don't want to lose. You have come this far because you were ready to let go of things. Stay aware of that fact.

2. SEEK BALANCE

Your visual identity system becomes an ensemble inside of the larger brand orchestra. Since your visual identity will have so many individual, front-facing components, give careful regard to a balanced approach. Similar to not expecting a logo to embody everything your brand represents, you need to spread the load around across elements.

Listen to your agency when they advocate for balance. I always direct clients to avoid doubling up on too many components and explain that they should feel comfortable spreading the story out a bit. Your new color palette, typography, logo, and pattern don't need to exude the same core attribute. You don't have to splash your new brand pattern on every web page, billboard, and sales deck.

Balance might sound counterintuitive, but I assure you it's a strong formula. Consider three brand attributes from a hypothetical comms phase: sophisticated, imaginative, and sincere. Your typography could be a minimalist sans-serif typeface that represents your "sophisticated" attribute. Meanwhile, your color palette boldly breaks the norm to represent "imaginative." As for "sincere," maybe it doesn't show up at all in the design but comes across in verbal and written components.

Salesloft, a client of ours, leaned into "sincere" (one of their voice attributes) as a way to balance their genuine spirit and their best-in-class B2B position. They went further into "sincere" with the help of custom photography as a way to demonstrate that being best in class and also authentically human are not mutually exclusive in a brand.

My main point is to use everything you have as you spread the load across the sum of your assets. What does Apple's logo express? Evolution? Nonconformity? Approachability? I'm not sure how they define it, but they surely aren't using it to express cutting edge tech. Their product imagery does that; therefore, the logo doesn't have to. When you spread out the intentionality of your design system, you avoid looking single faceted and successfully show the depth of your brand.

3. MEASURE VISUAL DESIGN AGAINST STRATEGY, GOALS, AND YOUR CUSTOMERS

Review the goals you've been working toward since the start, and ask your agency how design concepts derive from strategy. Do the designs align? How well do they serve the interests of your customers? For instance, what is logo version A trying to say? Is it doing so more successfully than version B?

Also ask your agency to provide insight into their rationale and inspiration behind various design decisions. What did they uncover during the strategy phase that led them in this direction? How well does it align with insights you've shared along the way, especially between iterations and rounds? Use this same criteria and way of thinking as the process continues, especially as your agency presents additional visual aspects (typography, visual language, etc.).

Ideally, your agency will be able to answer your questions in ways that help you understand the journey from their perspective. As they explain their thinking, they might also help you reframe your own, which can support future reviews. This can lead to new questions. For instance:

- How does the photography style align with your strategic brand attributes?
- How do these elements reflect the brand narrative taking shape in comms?
- How do these visuals take us closer to how we wish to be perceived?

4. IT'S RARELY LOVE AT FIRST SIGHT

Early visual renderings will not be "perfect," and your new amazing logo will not magically appear at the first attempt. There are a few reasons why:

- This is a cumulative, slow-building process. Each step brings you closer to the desired outcome. Hunt for progress week to week.
- You are not the intended audience—your customers are. Resist your natural reactions, remove personal tastes from the equation, and put yourself in their shoes using recommendations and directions from strategy.
- It's amazing what time plus context can do. Think of Nike again. They were originally named Blue Ribbon Sports.

When Phil Knight saw Carolyn Davidson's swoosh, he famously said, "I don't love it, but I think it will grow on me."[15]

- True love takes time. The designs you see in this process are for your new brand, not your current one. Be sure to treat them fairly.

Here's a quick anecdote from my personal vault: As a branding agency co-owner with a design background, I can assure you that I struggled with this very issue during the Focus Lab rebrand. I could not stop overthinking the logo. My desire to land on something legendary blurred the reality of what was actually important. I was more concerned with hitting a visual home run based on my own feelings than I was on defining a system that spoke to our customers and pushed our company forward.

Luckily I remembered the strategy, which kept reminding me of the same things I've shared throughout this chapter. Plus my business partners were great about steering our collective thinking. Give yourself some grace, and do your best to recall this point when the time comes.

THE WRAP ON VISUAL DESIGN

The visual design phase is a reminder that plenty of alchemy happens when you take conceptual ideas about identity and convey them in visible form in a way that people will *get it*. From that perspective, visual design has tremendous power and value and helps the brand speak volumes without saying a single word.

---

15   Paul Feldwick, "Brand = Image," *Admap* (March 2014): 20–22, http://paulfeldwick.com/wp-content/uploads/2017/04/Brand-equals-Image.pdf.

Part of measuring expectations and perspectives related to visual design involves appreciating all the work that got you to this point: early strategy, discovery, writing, visual strategy, and finally the design itself. Ideally, your agency will apply a great deal of empathy and understanding to this dynamic task. This is where partnering with an agency that cares as equally about the intangibles as they do the creative output really shows up.

As design wraps up, your comms work will too. This is a critical transition moment, and I've dedicated the entire next chapter to discussing it. Before I take us there, key takeaways from Part 3 follow.

PART 3 TAKEAWAYS

CHAPTER 6 TAKEAWAYS

A well-done strategy clarifies the core components of your brand's identity.

- There are three main legs to the strategy process: research, evaluation, and direction.
- Brand strategy direction should serve as a reference document for anyone creating on behalf of your brand.
- You have to uncover all the questions before you can provide a complete answer to a problem.
- Without a thoughtful strategy, your rebrand is just creativity for creativity's sake—devoid of meaning and lacking connection to your company's ethos.
- Market research literally cannot give you the answers to branding questions. Be prepared to think deeply about the brand problem you face throughout the strategy phase.

CHAPTER 7 TAKEAWAYS

In a brand sense, comms refers to brand writing and leads toward producing the verbal components of identity.

- Be mindful of the difference between "messaging" and "messages."
  - Messaging refers to the words and concepts required to define your brand identity. This *is* brand writing.
  - Messages are the words that communicate your identity to the world. These *are derived from* brand writing and are more aligned with marketing than with brand.
- The brand writing process covers the following:
  - Positioning and differentiation
  - Core messaging (purpose, mission, vision, values)
  - Unique selling proposition and value proposition
  - Audience messaging
  - Brand voice
  - Brand story
  - Style
  - Concepts and expressions
- As you review deliverables during the comms phase, your team must align on your core components of identity as well as the way you wish to communicate these components.

CHAPTER 8 TAKEAWAYS

To create a sound and successful visual design, the process must be rooted in strategy and accurately represent your identity.

- Logo doesn't matter as much as many people think it does (but it still matters).
- It benefits you and your team when you understand various

decision-making tendencies. This insight helps you make informed, strategic decisions. Some places where you'll run into this during design involve the following:

- Placing too much importance on logo
- Placing too much emphasis on differentiation
- Playing things too safe
- Trying to say too much with a single element

- Agencies take different approaches during design. Focus Lab's approach is to break design into two high-level phases: visual strategy and visual design.

  - Visual strategy bridges the written, theoretical work of strategy and comms and the practical manifestations of design.
  - Visual design begins once we have clear direction for next steps (following visual strategy).

- Keep in mind that there's no such thing as love at first sight. During visual design, iteration and review remain key.

PART 4

CHAPTER 9

THE HANDOFF

With all the excitement of having a shiny new brand in hand, the agency-to-client handoff is vitally important to a successful rebrand journey. In too many cases, it gets overlooked. Managing the finer pieces of a handoff with precision and intention will dramatically impact the ultimate success of the rebrand. I'm going to use this chapter to highlight why this phase is important, what happens, and how to ensure success.

I'd like to use an example from retail to illustrate what happens when you rush a launch of any kind. In 2013, the Target Corporation was setting up for an international expansion. They wanted to build off of their recent U.S. growth and capture interest in the Canadian market. They had everything in place to do so, including leadership, strategy, staff, stores, infrastructure, and technology.[16] Yet less than two years from their launch date, all Target Canada had to show were losses, including bil-

---

16   Joe Castaldo, "What Really Happened at Target Canada: The Retailer's Last
      Days," *McLean's*, January 21, 2016, https://www.macleans.ca/economy/business/
      what-really-happened-at-target-canada-the-retailers-last-days/.

lions of dollars, 17,000 employees, and the reputation of Target Corporation itself.

Was there a fatal flaw? Actually, there were many. No matter which one led to the biggest quantifiable loss, they all stemmed from having placed unrealistic expectations and time frames around things that were most critical. Their overzealous time horizon led to bad technology decisions, error-filled processes, poor hiring decisions, huge logistical errors, and more. Plus many of their issues compounded because Target Canada's leadership failed to acknowledge them as problems in the first place. They had their sights set on big, shiny, noteworthy goals; they failed to solve the on-the-ground issues that eventually undermined their success. The moral of this story, in relation to your rebrand journey: Take the time to do things right at this phase of your rebrand. The alternative could be devastating.

APPROACHING THE HANDOFF

"Can you send me our awesome new logo file? I want to print up some shirts for a few people on our team?" Some version of this question usually comes a few weeks before a rebrand project wraps. I actually love this question because of what it implies between the lines. It's a clear indicator that the brand is coming to life, and excitement is riding high. This question always comes from a position of extreme joy. After months of hard work, thoughtful critique, and deep collaboration, the fruits of our combined labors are in reach. Although it pains me to say it, my answer is always, "Sorry, not yet." I can feel the air slip out of the balloon as soon as I reply.

I get it. It feels like the work is done. You've landed on your assets, you've got visions of swag and ads, and you feel ready to go forward. Here are some things to consider:

- What might look done to you is not technically ready to use.
- Even when the assets are technically ready for use, you want things to roll out together, not piecemeal.

So, what does "technically ready to use" actually mean?

THE DIFFERENCE BETWEEN LOOKING AND BEING FINISHED

In Chapter 8, I shared a list of design assets you can expect to receive and review during the design phase. Just because you've seen a number of "approved" or "completed" assets doesn't mean you have everything you need to use them. As with the Target Canada story, without all the pieces working the right ways, the last thing you want to do is march into the world and start making it up as you go. Before you use anything in the wild, a few final steps must take place:

- Every asset needs to be polished. Your agency will consider variations such as different background colors, document variations, and use cases.
- All assets must be organized into a logical file structure to make it easy for you and your team to find what you're looking for.
- Final files must be exported into a single folder that will eventually become the folder your team uses.
- All assets plus documentation notes must be displayed and included in a final style guide.

What happens if your agency skips these steps or if you grow impatient before these final details are finished? Perhaps you've worked in a company or organization where some of the following are true:

- You need a logo file, but there are three different versions in the company hub. Which one do you use?
- The color palette on the pitch deck is different from what you use on the website, and it's not even close.
- Someone pulls the logo file, but it doesn't fit the marketing piece they're working on. No problem, they just stretch it into place. Better yet, they save their altered (incorrect) file in the company hub. No confusion at all.
- You have no idea what your company typeface system is or where to find it, so you just find something "similar" on your computer and go to town.

Maybe similar issues led to the inflection points that drove you to this book. Sadly, situations like these can happen right out of the gate when a rebrand handoff does not follow a deliberate and organized process.

POLISHING DESIGN ASSETS FOR SHIPMENT

Since so much about the rebrand experience is iterative, you will have seen your color palette, logo, typography, and other assets countless times. Ideally, you will have gone from a collection of loose ideas to a tightly wound and highly organized system. Along this path of changes and evolution, from large and sweeping modifications to razor thin tweaks, you've gotten to the "final" rounds. At that point, iterative questions will begin to sound like "Should this edge be rounded at .25 percent or .15 percent?" or "Should this red have 1 percent more vibrancy than the other red?" The thing is, all of these final adjustments need to be wrapped up before your assets are ready to use.

As iterations get laser focused, it's easy to lose sight of big picture decisions as well as technical aspects involved in having a body of ready-to-roll assets. Your agency is in charge of keeping track of these issues and making sure everything is executed correctly and consistently at the time of handoff.

The key takeaway here is: even though you've made a lot of concrete decisions about logo, color, type, etc., and you're over the moon about bringing this new brand public, you must allow space for some final attention to detail if you want to walk away with a successful brand system. To help you do so without getting too lost in the weeds, I want to offer some high-level considerations.

Considerations for Your Logo

Even after you've signed off on the logo, what orientations do you need for social media, print, trade shows, etc.? This is the moment when various marketing needs can surface in the brand project. Do you have horizontal and vertical orientations of your new mark and logotype? Are all the anchor points of the vector shape built accurately? What file types (.eps vs. .ai) do you need? Questions like these will be addressed in the work process, but this stage allows you and your agency time to catch any loose ends.

Considerations for Color

Color is a fickle beast. It all starts with the differences between screen color formats (RGB, Hex) versus printing codes (CMYK, Pantone). It's also essential to consider accessibility, which means accounting for people with sight impairments for whom certain visual elements will be difficult to distinguish. This phase allows for one final check to make sure every asset uses the same color formats and codes. It's easy for even the most trained eyes to miss certain color details. Taking time to make sure they're right across all assets is necessary.

Considerations for Typography

Typography has a unique position in this part of the project. This asset is actually a purchase on the client side. Your agency should tell you exactly what to buy and how to buy it. Then you will be responsible for downloading and storing these assets. Purchasing fonts directly means you have the original font license, which eliminates the unnecessary step of your agency having to transfer the license to you. It also allows you to retain your own account with the type foundry in case you need support or future downloads.

Considerations for Photography

Photography also holds a unique position in the handoff process. You will find yourself in one of two scenarios: using licensed photography, which would then follow the same licensing process as typography, or hiring a custom photographer for things like headshots, product photography, or broader culture and customer imagery. For either route, this phase allows your designers to capture style definitions and guidelines for future photography needs. If you take the custom photography route, once your designer has built out these guidelines in the style guide (more on this shortly), your photographer will use style definitions to build out a custom set of images for your needs.

POLISHING COMMUNICATIONS ASSETS

As your agency polishes these design components, the writer is wrapping up and packaging your communications assets and guidelines. As with design, you will also have reviewed dozens of written and verbal pieces of communication as part of the brand process. Now you must wait for the final, polished assets and guidelines to be ready before you can put them to use as a part of an intentional rollout.

Here's an important note about final comms components: These outcomes, like the work itself, are usually best received by someone with a writing or communications background. If you don't already have someone on your core project team with this expertise, it'll be helpful to enlist them now.

HANDOFF COMPONENTS

The handoff is an exercise in shared responsibility between you and your agency. They need to take the right amount of time to review all assets with a fine-toothed comb and then organize everything in a way that is manageable for you. The core deliverables in the handoff process include your brand style guide, communications style manual and assets, and all of your visual design files (sometimes numbering in the high hundreds).

Once delivered, you and your team will be set up to execute

consistently on your new brand. In most cases, there will be at least one live handoff meeting in which you and your agency review these components together. I'd like to cover each of these core deliverables as well as what to expect during the handoff meeting.

BRAND STYLE GUIDE

Your brand style guide will contain all aspects of your new brand identity, visual and verbal. This is your number-one deliverable and, ultimately, the holy grail of your entire project. This highly specialized and detailed document, often in excess of a hundred pages, covers your foundational verbal and visual assets as well as the "rules" related to executing on your new brand.

Every agency structures brand style guides a little differently. If you're working with Focus Lab, you can expect to find the following in your final brand style guide:

- Foundational brand identity elements, including attributes, core messages, and values, plus general guidelines for usage.
- Communications elements like voice and tone, value proposition, unique selling proposition, and brand story, plus general guidelines for usage.
- Visual elements including logo, color, typography, and art direction, plus specific guidelines for usage.

Let me come back to the word "rules," which I put in quotes above. There's a point of confusion worth calling out, and it's this: your style guide cannot and will not answer every question your team will encounter when designing on behalf of the new brand. It's not meant to. However, it is meant to capture elements that are foundational to your identity and to guide you in using them consistently wherever you use them. From this perspective, your guide holds the assets you'll use and the rules you'll want to follow as long as these assets remain in place.

At the same time, your brand is a living and evolving organism. It requires a certain amount of flexibility to thrive. You may find that you need to extend your color palette for the web down the road. Or your marketing team will need to create a variation of a pattern to use within an email template. In this way, the brand guide should leave room for interpretation, and the rules should be flexible enough to accommodate future needs.

Because of the confusion between branding and marketing and because this topic comes up very frequently, I want to double down on the fact that your style guide is not meant to give you specific answers to marketing questions. For instance, while it will synthesize and spell out your voice and tone, it will not provide specific verbiage for your next sales deck or an upcoming social media campaign.

As I mentioned in Chapter 7, you might fall in love with your brand positioning and wind up using a version of it on your website. That type of marketing direction is beyond the scope of your style guide. This and many other marketing elements are things you'll either create in-house, or will generate with the help of a marketing firm. (You might also work with your brand agency to create key marketing elements, which I'll discuss in Chapter 10.)

BRAND COMMUNICATIONS STYLE MANUAL AND ASSETS

In addition to the verbal identity components that are already in your brand style guide, most projects also result in some additional communications assets that accompany that style guide. Different agencies treat this content in a number of ways. At Focus Lab, we separate out detailed verbal style directives into a distinct communications style manual.

This manual is a customized ("house") version of one of the established industry style guidelines such as AP, Oxford, MLA, etc. You'll find a detailed direction on how to employ your brand voice and tone plus tailored guidelines that derive from an industry style manual. The communications style manual also includes word lists and terminology that reflect language you plan to use and which you wish to avoid.

Focus Lab also separates out all communications assets (verbal components of identity plus any messages we create based on these components) into a quick-reference format. We want to present you with something that your in-house writers can use quickly and effectively. It's a super simple collection of communications components involved in your project's scope, including things like your purpose, mission, vision, value proposition, unique selling point, audience messaging, brand story, and more.

Since these items also appear in your brand style guide, it's important that any evolutions or changes to this content show up in both places. Focus Lab ensures that this content matches at handoff. Once these documents are in your hands, someone on your team will own this job.

GETTING THINGS RIGHT THE FIRST TIME

Expect your agency to treat your style guides, manuals, and brand assets like the most important things on earth. Also expect them to keep these assets close until they're officially and finally ready to make their way into your hands. If your agency delivers a set of assets and even one color code or word is off, and then you distribute this asset, your successful rollout can get messy fast.

You should also expect your agency to present final assets in a way that's organized and easy to use. If you need help, your agency should be ready to guide you through accessing and transferring, navigating, and using different files and file types. For instance, the logo file alone may export into more than a hundred unique file types (black and white, full color, all white, all black, etc.). For some brands, this number will be upwards of a thousand files, depending on the various colors and design elements that make up the final logo and mark. That number might shock you—it shocks me too. As the adage goes, measure twice, cut once.

THE HANDOFF MEETING

Needless to say, your agency will be handing you a whole lot of pages and assets. When they do, it should happen in the most organized way possible, ideally via a live handoff meeting, which can take about an hour or so. If that's not explicitly stated in your project timeline, ask your agency to set this meeting up.

Handoff meetings make nice touchpoints, particularly among people who weren't heavily involved in the actual project but will be involved in the execution of the brand. Among those present should be your agency's designers, writers, and other team members who can answer questions about your assets and how to use them. The return on knowing how to use your assets properly and consistently is more than worth everyone's time.

This meeting is another example of when the difference between branding and marketing can come up. Whoever you take to that handoff meeting, it'll be helpful to make sure they're not expecting marketing direction as an outcome.

I haven't talked much about how interactive (web design/product design) factors into this process, but if interactive is a part of your rebrand process, expect a separate, specific design-to-development handoff. This meeting is a chance for your agency's interactive designers to review their designs with the development team, whether in-house or from a different agency. This meeting is particularly important for communicating UX expectations, motion and interactivity ideas, and any other development considerations that came up during the design process.

THE WRAP ON THE HANDOFF

Resist the urge to look at this handoff work as less important or to think that the work of your core project team is done. As your agency moves into refining assets, you should actually be using these guidelines and thinking about how to deputize members of your team to prepare for taking possession of these assets and guidelines and ultimately rolling them out to the world. Identify who on your team should be accountable to these steps and how to bring others from your organization into the process so that you can avoid the pitfalls of rushing your rollout (more on this in the next chapter).

Remember the Target example. Your company has invested a ton of time, money, and human capital in your rebrand. Just because the handoff is focused on details and documentation rather than creative doesn't mean it can't have a very real impact on your ability to realize a return on your investment. It could literally mean the difference between success and failure.

Speaking of the rollout, that's the last detail to cover, including steps like auditing the array of marketing assets you'll need to update ahead of your launch, building your rollout team and plan, and much more. These elements require a significant amount of effort, and someone will need to own and coordinate this process. Let's move to Chapter 10 and help you dial in these critical details before you launch.

CHAPTER 10

ROLLOUT AND LAUNCH

You finally have a brand system that truly represents your organization in the way it deserves. You now have perfected assets and guidelines in hand. Congratulations to all involved! Your strategic brand vision has never been clearer, your language exemplifies your organization's value in a unified way, and your design system accurately expresses everything visually and verbally. Now comes the final steps in maximizing the success of your rebrand project: your brand rollout and launch.

The rollout is a celebration. More importantly, it's a unique and delicate moment to share your new story with the world. When you approach and execute your rollout with intention, the experience can accelerate the impact of your rebrand significantly, right out of the gate. But if you approach it haphazardly, you might never tap into the greater value of the rebrand experience. In short, this is still very much a part of your rebrand, not a nice to have separate from the larger journey.

When Airbnb rolled out their new brand, they didn't say "Check out our new logo." They led with purpose by saying, "Imagine a world where you can belong anywhere," and pushed that narrative for months. This captured a different, more imaginative mindset. Instead of framing your rebrand as a design exercise, express it as a company-wide movement. This chapter will outline very clearly how to approach your rollout and capture the moment your new brand deserves.

APPROACHING ROLLOUT AND LAUNCH

"But why, some say, the moon? Why choose this as our goal? And they may well ask, why climb the highest mountain? Why, 35 years ago, fly the Atlantic? We choose to go to the moon in this decade and do the other things not because they are easy but because they are hard. Because that goal will serve to organize and measure the best of our energies and skills, because that challenge is one that we're willing to accept."[17]

—PRESIDENT JOHN F. KENNEDY, SEPTEMBER 12, 1962

If President Kennedy had said, "We've decided to send a space plane to the moon, I hope you like it," the speech would have barely made a blip. But because of the story he told and the way he told it, bringing us along in a quest for the betterment of humankind, his words represent a profound moment and remain in our collective consciousness. This is the energy and mindset to have when rolling out your brand.

Does this feel overdramatic? I hope not, because the point is

---

17 "Address at Rice University on the Nation's Space Effort," John F. Kennedy Presidential Library and Museum, accessed March 15, 2023, video, 18:27, https://www.jfklibrary.org/learn/about-jfk/historic-speeches/address-at-rice-university-on-the-nations-space-effort.

very real. Your rollout is a huge moment in the timeline of your organization. Treat it as such. Maximizing this moment will help you end up with brand devotees from the start. The entire rollout and launch experience involves building a series of smaller moments that send a powerful ripple across your team, customers, and vertical. It's a concerted effort that tells the world your company has doubled down on itself and is ready to reach new heights. This is a chance to clarify what your organization is building, explain why it matters, and stake your claim in a new space.

THE DIFFERENCE BETWEEN ROLLOUT AND LAUNCH

In practice, rollout and launch are intrinsically linked, though each follows its own cadence. Since many people use these terms interchangeably, I want to clarify how they overlap and how they're different.

Rollout involves all the steps that lead up to and follow your launch. This includes updating your legacy brand assets, and planning for when you'll make them available. Launch, on the other hand, refers to the moments you reveal your new brand and message to key internal and external audiences. What's more, you will have internal and external rollout activities as well as internal and external launches.

If you focus on launch only, you'll end up presenting your brand in a disorganized, inconsistent, and potentially damaging way. Instead, you should protect your launch as the unique and delicate moment it is—the first impression you'll only have one chance to make. To make it a lasting impression, a well-executed rollout is critical. Toward that end, I'll start with some mindset advice around getting ready for change and aligning around expectations. From there, I'll present a number of core elements to consider when approaching rollout and launch, including the following:

- When to begin planning your rollout (hint: much earlier than you might think).
- How to build your rollout team.
- The steps involved in auditing your existing assets.
- Knowing when to enlist outside support and/or vendors to produce assets.
- Targeting your launch date, and clarifying your message.
- Identifying your rollout audiences.
- Creating brand ambassadors.

As you review and follow the steps below, keep in mind that you should be thinking of your internal needs and audiences first. This will help ensure that your rollout and launch cocreate the most impact possible.

NO SNEAK PEEKS

It is going to be tempting to ease your fears about rollout by dripping pieces of the new brand to random colleagues in the weeks and months ahead of launch. Resist this temptation! There is a time and a method for sharing new brand elements as part of an organized rollout. Giving in to your excitement and forwarding the new logo around in an email thread or surprising someone by using any of the new brand assets out of context are quick trips down the very short road to a poorly received launch.

STAY FOCUSED ON CONSISTENCY

I've talked about the importance of consistency throughout this book. Make no mistake, it continues to matter during your rollout. Ultimately, consistency comes down to how well you plan timing and execution related to changing over from your old brand assets to the new system. You'll suffer from a disjointed and nonsensical rollout if any of the following occur:

- You make a big rebrand announcement on your website, but the website still embodies the old brand.
- You reveal any of your new brand publicly before you deliver your internal launch.
- Your social media does a great job of broadcasting the driving purpose behind your rebrand, but you haven't updated your product with any of the new brand's design system (i.e. color, type, etc).
- Your sales sheets and pitch decks continue to use old brand assets, even as new visuals make their way across your website and other material.

ALIGN EXPECTATIONS

During rollout, do not expect everyone to like everything they see. Remember how Phil Knight figured the swoosh would grow on him? The same might be true for some members of your internal and external audiences when you launch your updated brand. Not everyone will like it. It's uncomfortable to think about, but it comes with change. It's helpful to have realistic expectations so you're not tempted to react to criticism.

There is plenty you can do to protect against criticism, which is another function of the brand rollout. Don't let the idea of having critics internally or externally give you cold feet. Use it as motivation to create the best rollout plan you can, and stay a step ahead of their judgment. If you do so, you will have all the brand supporters you need.

Airbnb is a fantastic example of how building brand buy-in internally helps deflect external criticism. When they launched their brand refresh in 2014, they were met with an unimaginable amount of criticism.[18] Instead of responding angrily or scrambling to modify their logo, they doubled down on their rationale and retold the story of the Bélo as the universal symbol of belonging.[19] Then they backed it up with real-life stories from Airbnb hosts and guests. They leaned into the criticism and used it to build an even stronger story. When people see Airbnb's mark today, these past criticisms probably don't come to mind.

Here's a fun fact from the Focus Lab files: Within our client intake form, one question asks "What brands do you admire and why?" I can't tell you how many times we hear Airbnb mentioned in those answers. It literally feels like every other potential client lists them somewhere as a brand they admire. Use that knowledge to remind yourself that criticism does not mean a failed rebrand.

18   Jason Forrest, "The Airbnb Logo Redesign: Learning from the Controversy," *Digital Ink* (blog), June 16, 2022, https://www.digital.ink/blog/Airbnb-logo/.

19   Marion, "Airbnb's Consistent Rebrand Focuses on the Sense of Belonging to a Community," The Branding Journal, January 15, 2021, https://www.thebrandingjournal.com/2014/07/airbnbs-consistent-rebrand-focuses-sense-belonging-community/.

BEGIN PLANNING ROLLOUT EARLIER THAN EXPECTED

You cannot begin your rollout planning early enough. It's okay to set various aspects of your rollout for different times, but if you wait to start planning until after you receive your style guide, you will quickly realize that the amount of work ahead of you outpaces the time and resources at your disposal.

We direct our clients to begin thinking about their brand rollout before they see a single design deliverable. Consider that for a moment. You can imagine how early that might feel. I assure you, you'll want as much time as possible to plan your rollout. In fact, it's best to spread your efforts across months, not weeks. I recommend treating rollout like its own internal project, complete with its management and timeline. Let me be clear here: It will be your team's job to manage rollout. Your agency may advise and assist you, but your team owns this effort. When all is said and done, your rollout plan should clearly outline the following:

- Which internal and external assets you will update, and in what order.
- When, how, and where you'll introduce various assets.
- How the internal and external launches will happen.

Let's take a look at the details involved in executing on your rollout plan.

BUILD YOUR ROLLOUT TEAM

You'll want to get ahead of identifying your rollout team as soon as possible. In the same way that you made considerations around your internal rebrand project team (Chapter

4), you need to make similar decisions with your rollout team. Rely on a small, focused group that covers a cross section of your company and possesses the strengths and perspectives to execute.

Ideally, your project rebrand team is the rollout team, and team members take on core rollout responsibilities. You can also augment your core project team with a small rollout-specific team to bring some new energy and skills to the table. Either way, make sure your people are dedicated to key tasks and that new team members come up to speed on the new brand. Here are some of the core roles and responsibilities to consider:

- A detail-oriented professional to build and stay accountable to your rollout plan. This is basically a rollout owner or a PM.
- A leader on your team to manage the execution and timing involved in implementing new brand assets. This could be a design leader, comms leader, marketing leader, etc.
- A decision maker from the marketing team to determine and approve spending on anything related to your rollout budget.
- Someone from the product or service team who has intimate knowledge of customer-facing tools that need to be updated visually or verbally.
- Someone with close connections to customers who can leverage influential customer-side relationships for launch amplification.
- Someone to serve as a longer-term brand manager, ensuring that the new brand standards are upheld in the future.

Once again, it's never too early to begin building this team, but it definitely can be too late. Your rollout team will need a few months to tackle all the moving parts, so take care not to leave them with only weeks. In some cases, I've encouraged clients to begin building their rollout team as early as a few weeks into the project. Starting early gives you a chance to grasp the magnitude of the rollout effort so that you can adequately plan to accomplish key pieces before your launch date.

KNOW WHEN TO ENLIST OUTSIDE SUPPORT

Although our clients range in size, typically from Series A to pre-IPO, we hear the following two things repeatedly across the board when it comes to updating brand materials with the new assets:

1. "We don't have a big enough internal team (marketing, design, or comms) to update all of our brand assets. Do you know any freelancers?"
2. "We have people on the team who can do this work, but they are focused on other efforts right now. How should we handle this?"

If you find yourself in either of these situations, don't ignore it. Applying new brand assets across the entire board can be a huge effort. Before you start to dole out work to internal team members or look into local marketing or design shops for help, consider whether or not your brand agency is an option. Not every agency offers post-project support, but some do. Since Focus Lab offers rollout-specific support, I wanted you to know that it's an option to explore. If you want some outside help, here are some questions related to managing the full scope of your implementation:

- What do you need help with? Is it just applying the brand to rollout-critical assets? Do you need help figuring which assets to update as part of your rollout? Since agencies provide different levels of services, some will be more competent than others in specific areas. Clarify what you need first, then make sure any outside teams can provide the right solutions.
- Is your agency built to shift their focus from the iterative, creative design phase to an asset-specific one? If you need more creative work or more build-out of the brand, you might consider a follow-up creative project. However, if your core need involves extending your brand to various applications and mediums (marketing), then make sure your agency is set up to do so.
- Does your agency have a separate group that handles asset-related activities, or will you be working with the same team that worked on your core brand project? Creative projects feel different than asset production, and the team that rocked your rebrand won't necessarily create the same customer experience. Find out who you'll be working with, and make sure to set your expectations accordingly.
- How will the process unfold? Do you submit requests for work, or do you determine them collaboratively? Will you have a dedicated PM on your side? Or is it more of a ticketing process, where you will be uploading feedback and changes into a queue?
- What kind of turnaround time do you expect or need? If you're looking for rapid, in-the-moment turnarounds, make sure that's what your agency does. Often the fast-turnaround shops are not the ones to help you make strategic decisions about rollout needs and timing.
- Do you require a long-term engagement with a team that can fulfill your asset needs for an extended period of time?

If so, then your needs most likely extend beyond rollout and launch. Use this knowledge to help decide who to work with and when.

Whether or not you enlist the support of your current brand agency, leverage the strengths of your team, or hire a new firm, finalize your list of implementation needs as much as possible. This will help you plan for the right level of support.

IDENTIFY YOUR LAUNCH DATE

Setting a specific launch date helps you work backwards from the date as you plan each step that leads to it as well as the steps that come after. Sounds easy enough, right? Honestly, exact launch dates can be hard to nail down. Decisions tend to fall in one of two camps: you either have a specific event on the calendar that you're targeting or you're picking a date that feels realistic but isn't tied to a single event.

What kind of event marks an opportune launch date? That depends on your company. In Focus Lab's experience, companies like to plan launches around industry conferences, times of year that align with various sales cycles, or the release of a new product or service. It's a way to capitalize on preexisting buzz and pile on more excitement.

Still, you don't have to take this route, especially if you're not building toward a preexisting event or internal campaign. Instead, consider launching at a time that is traditionally quiet in your business or at a moment that would benefit from some excitement. No matter how you get there, work with your rollout team to determine your target date.

AUDIT YOUR ASSETS

Before you write your launch date down in ink, make sure that you have a clear picture of the assets you need to update. As you get ready to lock down the calendar, you need to determine the delivery of key branded assets, including the turnaround times for vendors plus your own strategy for implementing assets. There are a lot of intricacies involved in this planning, and I'll cover them in greater detail shortly. For now, focus on culling a list of any and all assets that reflect your brand. This list of assets will be long, and there will be many tasks involved in updating them. When you compile a complete picture of what needs to be updated and by when, you can firm up your launch date and give everyone enough time to make critical changes. Here are a few items to help get you started:

Digital Updates

- Your entire website
- Assets linked from your site (white papers, digital downloads, etc.)
- Your product UI
- Social media channels
- All sales and marketing templates (newsletters, presentations, etc.)
- Your email and other digital signatures
- White-labeled internal platforms
- Meeting backgrounds
- Podcasts or motion/video graphics or assets

Physical Updates

- Environments (trade show booths, banners, etc.)

- Signage in your office
- Document and deck templates, direct mailers, billboards
- Letterhead, business cards, recruiting materials
- Shirts, hats, and other swag

Bigger Assets to Consider

- How long will it take to get a new illuminated sign to hang on the side of your downtown building?
- How long before you can paint your entire office in the new brand colors?
- Will you have your new booth design in time for your big conference?
- Who's in charge of the new landing page that discusses the rebrand? What is the page going to say? Who is going to develop it?

From this list alone, you can see how a few weeks would never allow you to navigate a successful rollout.

CLARIFY YOUR LAUNCH NARRATIVE

Your launch narrative is your very own JFK moon shot address. When you frame your rollout within a compelling narrative, everyone—from your stalwart brand champions to your critics—will understand why your rebrand makes sense. You'll firmly plant all of the nuanced decision-making related to colors, words, and symbols into a larger narrative, which will help mute any instances of personal bias. Plus your rollout narrative will help build excitement for the upcoming reveal, making the whole thing feel like a curated, well-executed crusade. This point could not be more important.

- Your rollout story might come right out of your new brand story. That's what Airbnb did with theirs. They pushed on the idea of imagining a world where you can be anyone anywhere, and their rollout highlighted what they believed in and why it mattered.
- Your rollout narrative might communicate the purpose of your rebrand, sharing your pre-rebrand pain points, and showing your audience how you resolved them. For instance, if your biggest pain point was related to market position, this can be a compelling message to include in your rollout narrative. Or perhaps you'll want to build your rollout narrative around the fact that you are no longer a collection of M&A assets but a singular brand under a new name.

Regardless of your goals, decide what's at the core of your rebrand, and build your rollout narrative with intention. If you're going to make brand noise, make sure your noise has purpose. You can enlist your agency to craft your rollout narrative or write it internally. Either way, your rollout narrative will frame how you will ultimately present the brand internally and externally and can be one of the most compelling factors in building brand followers.

IDENTIFY YOUR ROLLOUT AUDIENCES

Many companies see the rollout and subsequent brand launch as being a singular moment. This is a shortsighted view. An experienced brand agency will tell you that your rollout has two distinct parts: sharing the new brand with your team (internal), and then sharing it publicly with everyone (external).

How much thought have you given to your internal launch?

How much impact will this have on whether or not your internal team members buy in? Have you thought about how your launch will happen for investors? Your board? You will also need to introduce these audiences to your new brand. Take the time you need to make sure that when they see it, however that is, the experience is inclusive of and makes sense to them. Plan each of these moments and interactions (along with their supporting assets) in a timeline, and give each of them their own attention.

CREATE BRAND AMBASSADORS

At this point, your rollout plan is nearly complete, but you need more than just the steps to follow. This is the moment where you must begin building brand champions internally. One way to start is by revealing and discussing the brand, drawing on your launch story with key individuals (internal influencers) before your formal internal launch.

To get started, meet with your internal rollout team first, then with auxiliary stakeholders who have been helping throughout the rebrand. There's definitely going to be an emotional pull that comes from multiple angles. Before you get lost in your ever-growing list of things to do, look for ways to motivate and align team members, and make sure everyone is moving in the same direction. That way, as the launch date gets closer, everyone will have a solid sense of their tasks and responsibilities and the role they play in the launch.

Enlisting brand champions before the broader internal launch is a way to bring other people along on the journey. It's a reminder that they play an important part in the rebrand's success. This gives you additional influential voices inside the company and doesn't leave the galvanizing to a single person.

Now that you have built your project team, found a launch date, audited your assets, clarified your narrative, identified your audiences, and deputized some internal brand ambassadors, you're ready to put your launch in motion.

LAUNCH

You are about to go live, and the world is ready to experience your new brand. I've spoken with many founders post-rebrand and asked them what the most rewarding moment in their entire rebrand experience was. By and large, "launch" is the answer I hear most frequently. Let's go through some of the details Focus Lab covers with our clients as they head into launch, starting with your internal launch.

INTERNAL LAUNCH

It is easy to think of your launch as a single event—a noise-making scenario where the world finds out collectively in one big splash. Let me guide you through a slightly different approach that will create a greater impact with your team and external reception of your rebrand. Step one is your internal launch: presenting your new brand to your company only. This is a milestone moment for your organization and requires its own level of attention.

Your team is the frontline of this new brand. They are the ones carrying the flag and delivering on the brand promise. Getting them aligned first is not only the respectful thing to do but creates the initial clarity and larger brand ambassadorship. This is a special moment within your organization to rally the troops.

As I've written, I can't count how often our previous clients share how rewarding the internal rollout was in their rebrand journey. Here are two examples from post-rebrand conversations:

Mike Massey, CEO @ Locally

We had an all-hands meeting and very few people knew what we were working on. At the end of the meeting I told everybody to open the box and we spent the next hour or so walking through the brand, the symbolism, the hidden meanings, etc. It was unbelievable to everybody. Then when we were able to finally implement some of the home page redesign, literally the first day, one of our biggest clients sent us a note on the side and said, "Your rebrand is insane."

Kent Siri, VP of Marketing @ Reify

We were announcing our Series B and that coincided with the rollout. I had an hour-and-a-half meeting with the team to deliver this rollout. What I tried to do in that brand rollout presentation was bring people through the process. I didn't open that call saying here's the new logo, tagline, and colors. It was actually a buildup over the course of an hour—walking through why we are doing this and why it is important. I showed screenshots of the exercises you all did. I put in screenshots of the strategic brief to show how much thought and strategy goes into a project like this so I could set the table for the ultimate reveal. Then seeing the reactions once we unveiled the brand and to see how excited people were—to see them understand how this rebrand is going to unlock so much from a sales perspective, a customer experience perspective, a communications perspective. That was incredibly gratifying.

These insights, along with others from this series, come as no surprise to me. Having experienced this myself during Focus Lab's rebrand, and having been a part of a few special client internal presentations, the internal rollout truly is a magic moment. Treat it as such. Here are some tips to help you maximize it.

Identify the Voice of the Rebrand

The voice of your rebrand needs to come from an extremely high and influential seat in the organization. Ideally, your CEO and/or founder will be the biggest voice in the internal rollout. Whoever it is, your project driver should be closely supporting them (assuming the voice is not the driver). This one-two punch will set the tone for the launch resonance you want in your organization. Remember at this point, it's not about the new colors or updated logo; it's about the greater recalibration of the business. This is the story you must share from the top, especially if you want your culture to buy into the mission. Let leadership set the tone.

Make it Special

This is a moment to really dial up the intention and passion within the business. A twenty-minute conference call with lazy slides is not what you're looking for. You want to find your version of JFK's momentous address.

Present Your Story

That brand story you've been building since the beginning of your project is going to set the tone of your presentation. You'll use that, combined with a few other key points to draft your presentation. The structure will look something like this:

- What stands in your way as a business?
- What is your vision of the future in this organization?
- How your old brand was holding back that vision.
- How you recognized it was time to invest in your future and rebrand.
- The strategic decisions that were made in your rebrand process.
- How you progressed through the process.
- The final brand outcome and how it supports the vision of the future.
- How important your team and your people are to your success moving forward.

Know How You Want to Gather

What makes sense for your organization when it comes to locations and budgets for your internal rollout? Some companies have small, fully distributed teams of less than forty people. Others have hundreds, even thousands of employees scattered among multiple offices. There is no one-size-fits-all approach when it comes to a successful internal rollout. If you've nailed the earlier points (message from the top voice, making it special, and telling a compelling story) you are going to do great, whether it's in person or online. Focus Lab has seen success in both approaches. The delivery, planning, tone, and contents matter more than the location.

Make it Memorable

You might find yourself second guessing whether the moment really requires a blowout party or if you can just grab a normal team meeting slot and deliver a quick overview. Remember your rebrand will have been a highly personal exercise, especially for members of your core team. While your eyes might be on the external launch, the people inside of your organization are your heart and soul. Make this an enjoyable experience for them as they get to discover the new vision and understand the thinking and process behind it. This will help them align with the new brand as they carry the flag forward. Give this moment and your people the energy and attention they deserve.

Leave Room for Training

Your internal launch is a powerful moment to train your team on the outcomes of the rebrand. Your sales team needs to understand any new language that may have changed. HR is going to need any updated core values or other culture-related statements that may have been revised. Think about all the touchpoints for your brand and the people that work with them every day. Be sure to include them in your rollout so people have what they need to understand and act on them.

PUBLIC LAUNCH

Now let's shift attention to your public (external) launch. Although the same mindset and similar functions from your internal launch will happen in your external launch, there are some additional points I'll make here. The actions that will be consistent across internal to external launches include the following:

- Lead with purpose and story.
- Create clarity on why this is happening and why now.
- Speak to what it means for the future and how your customers will benefit.
- Make this launch deeply rooted and make it come from the top.

Below I've outlined a few other actions that will help guide a successful public launch.

Build Hype by Teasing Some Noise

Leading up to your public launch is a good time to start building up a groundswell. How? To start, leverage your current customer base and broader network of investors, partner organizations, and even social followers with some version of a hype campaign. You can do this with great success, and without investing a ton of resources (people or financial), as a way to get people excited and build momentum toward your public launch.

Some of our clients have done this exclusively through social media channels. By teasing out unidentifiable visual crops of their new brand pattern, for example, they get interest brewing as the release date approaches. Often it takes place in stages, where the first post simply alludes to something on the horizon, and subsequent posts grow increasingly visual and story driven without fully spilling the beans by sharing the launch story and brand assets. This approach can drive interest and create a social conversation leading up the moment—and keep followers tuned in.

You can also build a fully fledged campaign that leads up to your launch. We've seen similar and effective campaigns from clients over the years. Salesloft is a good example. They cleverly called their approach the "What's in the Box?" campaign. This type of interest-driving campaign is essentially a box containing a surprise. Typically, the box holds some imaginative version of newly branded materials in a beautiful unboxing experience. What's powerful about this approach is the tangibility. Sending this box out to your best customers, industry influencers, and even your team will create an exciting way to create suspense. Recipients literally become part of the rebrand experience. When prompted, they're involved in unveiling the new brand. You can also build hashtags around this to drive social resonance.

Let Customers Know What's Coming

Before you send out mysterious boxes (or whatever route you take), make sure you consider the level at which you want customers to be privy to the rebrand. You want to avoid jarring them. To do so, consider the following:

- Is there a tier of customers you would like to "bring into the know" ahead of time? How much advance notice would they appreciate, and in what way?
- What partnering organizations should know about your rebrand early?
- Will your rebrand feel like a big shift to some people? (For instance, a new position in the market, a name change, new offering, etc.) Or will the rebrand feel less shocking but still impactful? Use the answer to this question to guide the story you share with them as well.

Answering these types of questions can help you determine additional steps you might take before your full public release.

Prepare Your Public Launch Logistics

The size and content of your public launch event depend on who you are, what you're trying to accomplish, and your budget. Regardless of the style and substance of the event, here are some logistics to consider and line up early on:

- Speakers and presenters
- The presentation itself
- Entertainment
- Swag and giveaways
- Post-event follow-up messages and announcements

Not every company announces their rebrand at an event. However you launch, make sure the experience aligns with the truth of your organization and who you are at your core.

Keep Making Noise

Your rollout doesn't stop after you make some noise with your launch. In fact, it could take months. Some organizations are able to make their public rollout feel like a flip of a switch. One day everything is one way, and then suddenly it's another. Even when it seems this way, these organizations are still updating assets behind the scenes. To their credit, they prioritized well and tackled the right elements first. This is the same outcome you should strive for.

Make as much change as possible heading into your launch, but don't fool yourself into thinking you'll be done with everything after the launch event. A successful and complete brand rollout can take months, perhaps up to a year. The key to success is in how well you prioritize every step.

Don't confuse this for thinking you can just update your homepage and then take six months to get everything else up to speed. That would be a disaster. Make a big dent across your largest touchpoints (web, product, social, etc.), then work your way toward the rarely seen documents over the following months.

BRAND BUILDING DOESN'T STOP AFTER YOU REBRAND

Back in Chapter 1, I wrote that the success of Nike's brand came after decades of powerful marketing. To this day, they continue to hit the high notes. In Chapter 2, I wrote about the power of consistency and what it means to stay with things over time. After you roll out and launch your rebrand, the long game of brand building begins.

The good news is that your brand has never been in better shape for success. Keep it top of mind. Appoint a brand keeper, brand manager, brand ambassador, or a whole brand tribe to help ensure a high level of consistency and eliminate brand debt in the process. Continue to see your brand as something worthy of investing in, and hold it to the same standards as you do your products, services, and customer support.

THE WRAP ON ROLLOUT AND LAUNCH

A poorly managed rollout will tamp out the fire you're trying to light under your launch, leading to a missed opportunity. The lasting consequences of a lackluster launch might even mean falling into the same trap or condition that put you in a position to rebrand in the first place.

Think of your rollout and launch as a multi-faceted strategic strike. This is a key time for your business to communicate why your mission and vision are important and what they mean. Don't worry about being too loud. In fact, now is not the time to be quiet. Let the world know that you've changed for the better, and that you believe in this new direction with all your heart. As you go, don't go alone. Bring your brand champions with you on this journey. Share the megaphone with people who care about your company and understand why this matters.

PART 4 TAKEAWAYS

CHAPTER 9 TAKEAWAYS

The agency-to-client handoff is one of the most critically important steps to the success of your entire rebrand experience.

- Just because something looks done doesn't mean it's ready to use.
- Never roll rebranded assets out piecemeal.
- Your new visual and verbal brand assets need to be polished and packaged correctly. At the same time, your guidelines must be locked in before you can use assets (no matter how badly you want to start sharing them).
- Expect your agency to provide complete visual and verbal guides.
- Resist the following temptations:
  - Using assets before they're polished.
  - Rushing the polishing period.
  - Running forward with using assets without established guidelines in place.

- Your brand style guide is the core deliverable during this phase. It includes:
  - Foundational brand identity elements (attributes, core messages and values, general guidelines for usage, etc.)
  - Communications elements (voice and tone, value proposition, unique selling proposition, brand story, plus guidelines for usage)
  - Visual elements (logo, color, typography, art direction, plus guidelines for usage)
- The brand communications style manual and associated assets is another core deliverable to be ready for.
  - It's typically a customized version of established industry style guidelines (such as AP, Oxford, MLA, etc.)
  - It will include instructions on how to employ your brand voice and tone plus tailored guidelines.
  - It will also include word lists and terminology that reflect language you plan to use as well as words/phrases to avoid.

CHAPTER 10 TAKEAWAYS

It's never too early to plan your rollout or launch. Don't be afraid to discuss this with your agency early in the rebrand process.

- Where dates are concerned, pick realistic ones. Once in place, you can work backwards as you plan, make updates, and prepare critical assets for launch.
- To get ready for your rebrand rollout, consider the following questions:
  - What internal and external assets will you update and in what order? You absolutely want to be clear on what

needs to be updated (website, sales decks, product UI, office decor, etc.).

- When, how, and where will you introduce various assets?
- How will internal and external launches happen?
- Building your rollout team is just as important as building your internal rebrand team. Look to fill the following roles:
  - A detail-oriented professional to build and stay accountable to your rollout plan (your rollout "owner" or PM).
  - A leader to manage the execution and timing involved in implementing new brand assets. (This could be someone from design, comms, marketing, etc.)
  - A decision maker to determine and approve spending on anything related to your rollout budget.
- Be mindful of when and how to bring in third-party support (whether it's your existing brand agency or another vendor you vet and trust).
- When it's time to launch, plan your internal launch first, then your public launch.
- Be ready to get pushback from employees who don't like the change. Give them the insight and tools they need to get on board. Criticism isn't necessarily a bad thing. It could just be a symptom of change.
- Don't be afraid to overplan where various messaging details are concerned. As you create noise, you want to do so strategically.
- Brand building doesn't stop with your rollout and launch. These moments might represent the end of your rebrand journey, but they signal the start of the long road of brand building.

CONCLUSION

Have you ever looked at another company and wondered, "How did they get where they are? What's their magic? Why do people align so strongly to their brand?" I can't help but consider this question over and over again. As I do, I also consider my own experience with their brand. How have I changed? I used to love them when I was younger...why not now? Is it them or me? Why do I suddenly love this company that's been around forever but that I barely noticed until a year ago? Again, what's changed?

My point is that brands give us these kinds of opportunities. They are out there for public consumption, however we wish to consume them. Sometimes, they are stubbornly static. Other times, they change overnight. There's a story in the news. A shakeup. A scandal. They fall short on a promise, or they alter their promise, put out a new message, and forget about everything they said two years ago.

Even though a great deal of brand success comes down to consistency, there's nothing more consistent in business, or in life for that matter, than change. With change comes reinvention. As I wrap this book up, I want to be sure to touch upon this very topic.

While your rebrand is about changing your outward-facing appearance, if what's happening on the inside is working (related to your culture, people, and ethos), then this should remain the same. The process of getting to the outward execution involves strategy, emotion, and execution. It needs to be practical and tactical at every phase. It has to take the question of "What is a brand?" and reconfigure it to read, "What is *our* brand?" If you already have that answer, then you should be able to convey the importance of your brand to others in your company. If you can't, or if they can't grab hold of it, then perhaps this gap is where your own rebrand needs to start.

If you're considering a rebrand, then perhaps there's some discord between what your company is and how it seems to be, or at least how it showcases itself. Something about the DNA of your company isn't getting through. That's where a successful rebrand can make a world of difference. When done correctly, and with the right partner, a rebrand can be one of the most effective and powerful ways in which your company can create new energy and turn a slack tide into a wave of powerful momentum.

ARE YOU READY FOR YOUR REBRAND?

You may have already decided that your company needs a rebrand, perhaps even based on something you read in this book. That's great. But need and readiness are two different things. Here's a final checklist to help you determine if your company is actually ready:

DO YOU HAVE A VISION OF THE FUTURE?

Your agency can help you refine and define the answers to many things, but you can't expect them to provide a plan for where your business is headed. You will want some version of this vision to exist, even if it's cloudy, before you begin your rebrand. Your agency can hold up a mirror and say, "This is what we see and hear." From this, you can determine how disconnected your brand is from the vision you're chasing. With this in mind, if you have strong internal disagreements about the future vision of your business, resolve them before you embark on a rebrand. Doing so will simplify your rebrand efforts. In the process, this will further clarify your vision and even cement it into place.

ARE THE RIGHT PEOPLE ALIGNED AND ASSIGNED INTERNALLY?

Do you currently have the right mix of people to meet the demands of a rebrand? Do you have buy-in and support to get the resources you will need to make your rebrand a success? Make a short list of people already in alignment as well as those you'll have to sway. How will you communicate your plans to get their support? Use the recommendations I've shared in this book to help people understand that the challenges your company is facing are related to your brand and that you'll need their help to solve them. Go so far as to let them know the roles they'll play in the rebrand itself.

DO YOU KNOW WHAT TO LOOK FOR IN AN AGENCY?

Everything that happens during a successful rebrand involves a give and take between you and your agency. I spent a lot of time writing about our agency. My intent was to shine a light on the things you'll need to consider when evaluating potential rebrand partners. Taking on a rebrand and working with a brand agency are not things that most people do every day. I hope this book has helped clarify your thinking and given you new tools you can use to pick the right agency partner.

LAST THOUGHTS ON *CONQUERING YOUR REBRAND*

The job of branding, and of rebranding, has very little to do with whether or not you *personally* like or love the new brand. Instead, it's about how well the brand will play out in the world and in the vision of where you want your company to go. The work is never about you. It's about something bigger.

If you're ready to engage in a rebrand, take this note to heart: There will be parts of the process that you'll enjoy, parts you won't, and parts that land somewhere in between. Do your best to trust the process.

Chances are, you already know what you need to do next. You've known from the moment you picked up this book. Heck, you probably knew it before you picked up this book. Maybe you wanted the book to appease that nagging voice in your head that was saying "But we're just not ready," or "It's too risky." Maybe you wanted extra details and confirmation from a group that has done this successfully countless times.

Success in the rebrand journey favors the well prepared. There will be hiccups and hitches, but I bet you're more prepared for them now than you were at the start of this book. Or if you've already started a rebrand and you're stuck, don't be afraid to consult this book. It might help you find your way.

To borrow some language from Bob Moore, who was kind enough to write the foreword, my hope is that this book read like an "extended case study for how, when, what, and why" to engage in a rebrand, and not like a sales pitch. Don't get me wrong, we're open for business, but my main goal has been to educate, demystify, and promote the potential of brand and branding in a way that makes you feel like the transformational power of a rebrand is well within your reach.

ACKNOWLEDGMENTS

First and foremost, I want to thank my wife. The encouragement and grace you gave me throughout an entire year as I sat endlessly typing in this old brown chair means everything. It's not lost on me what it must be like to be married to an entrepreneur who loves his job and gives it a ton of attention. Adding a book to the mix meant even more time, which turned into late nights and weekends. Your selflessness gave me the space to feed my ambitions, and for that, I'm extremely grateful.

Tackling this book was as rewarding and exhausting as I thought it might be. Having said that, if it were not for my Scribe, Dave Jarecki, and the amazing team at Scribe Media, this book would still be a distant dream and not resting in the readers' hands. Thank you, Dave, for spending an entire year with me. You were a fantastic collaborator, and similar to the rebrand journey we take our clients on, you were the shepherd I needed on my book journey.

Although I co-founded Focus Lab and have played a critical

role in so many aspects of our business, this book and the level of detailed insights throughout it would not be possible without Shabnam Gideon, currently our strategy director. She understands Focus Lab, our process, our clients, and the rebrand journey at such a deep level it was essential to pull her into this writing process. Without her close partnership in this book, it wouldn't be what it is today. Her attention to detail, structure, and the reader's perspective made this book clearer and more impactful. Without her, I'd still be sitting in this brown chair, plucking away at the keyboard. Thank you Shabnam.

At Focus Lab, we believe in the power of an intentionally built team and leveraging the unique strengths of each individual for the best result. This book is a prime example of that. Thank you to everyone on the book team inside Focus Lab. Each of you brought your unique abilities and made the overall outcome that much better, and more enjoyable, I might add.

First off, to Haley Bridges for your strategic mind, using your superpower of research and discovery to help provide supporting data and psychology. Making this book more than loose opinions and theories.

To Justin Sims, PM extraordinaire, for helping to manage all the tasks, organize all the meetings, and keep this train rolling.

To Stetson Finch and Bud Thomas, for your design talents, elevating the book design and landing page to a place I couldn't have achieved.

To Genina Ramirez, Charisse Bennett, Natalie Kent, and Stephanie Taylor-Coleman, for your expert eyes on the chapters that aligned most closely with your expertise at Focus Lab.

To Liz Kelley for managing the long list of marketing touch points and outcomes on this book effort.

Writing a book is one thing; building a business is another. A giant thank you to my two business partners, Erik Reagan and Will Straughn. There would be no reason to even consider writing this book if it weren't for the powerful business we've built and the lessons we've learned together. Thank you for trusting me to represent the company in such a special way.

Going further, thank you to each and every Focus Lab team member, past and present. I stand on your shoulders in writing this book. The learnings and perspectives that fill these pages are a result of working side by side, day after day, with each of you. You embody the values, drive the mission forward, and never stop at the chance to make what we do better, even when that is hard. Thank you for your devotion. You all have shaped me and this book more than you know.

A special thank you to Bob Moore for taking the time to write such an authentic, transparent foreword for this book. I speak for our whole team when I say it's been a pleasure working with you multiple times now, and proud to have played a part in your journey from brand skeptic to brand evangelist.

Finally, thank you to all of our clients. You inspire the team and me to reach new heights and find ways to serve you better year after year. Thank you for allowing us to live out our mission. Stepping in to work side by side with you and your team to unlock the full potential of your organization is why we get out of bed. Conquering a rebrand starts and ends with trust. Thank you for trusting Focus Lab.

ABOUT THE AUTHOR

BILL KENNEY is an accomplished CEO and entrepreneur with a wealth of experience in the branding industry. He is the co-founder and CEO of Focus Lab, a global B2B branding agency that helps organizations lead their industries through the power of brand.

With a proven track record of success and a passion for design and entrepreneurship, Bill has earned a reputation as a leading figure in the world of branding. His company has been sought out by some of the most successful B2B companies in the world, including Marketo, Salesloft, Zuora, Braze, Outreach, Launch-Darkly, Twilio, Adobe, ASAPP, Luminate, Netflix, and Shopify, among others.

Growing up on Martha's Vineyard, Massachusetts, Bill Kenney was surrounded by the beauty of nature, which nurtured in him a deep appreciation for the outdoors. Despite being known as a popular vacation spot for the wealthy, the island has a strong blue-collar work ethic, which has had a profound impact on

Bill's character and values. He was raised with a strong sense of determination and hard work. This continues to influence his leadership style, instilling in him a great sense of humility and respect for the world around him.

Bill's academic journey reflects his passion for creativity. He pursued a degree in fine arts from the University of Tampa, Florida, where he developed his skills and gained valuable insights into the world of visual expression and design. After earning his BFA, Bill landed in the quiet southern city of Savannah, Georgia, intending to pursue a master's degree at the Savannah College of Art and Design. Although that vision changed upon arrival, his unwavering commitment and passion for design ultimately led him to co-found Focus Lab.

Bill Kenney's leadership and expertise extend beyond his role at Focus Lab. As a member of the Fast Company Executive Board, he shares his insights and knowledge with other business leaders. His Enneagram 2 personality type reflects his love for people. He believes that success is not just about achieving personal goals but also about serving others and helping them succeed. His commitment to serving others is evident in his work with this team as well as other entrepreneurs and business owners, where he offers guidance and support to help them reach their full potential. He remains committed to making a positive impact in the branding industry and beyond.

In his free time, Bill enjoys spending time outdoors or pursuing new hobbies. Running, reading, and camping are among his favorite activities, providing him with a much-needed break from the fast-paced world. He currently resides in New Jersey with his wife and son, where they enjoy exploring the great outdoors in their camper and spending quality time together as a family. Bill's commitment to work-life balance and his love for nature reflect his belief in the importance of taking care of oneself, staying grounded, and finding joy in the simple things in life.

Made in United States
Troutdale, OR
09/06/2023

12667969R00148